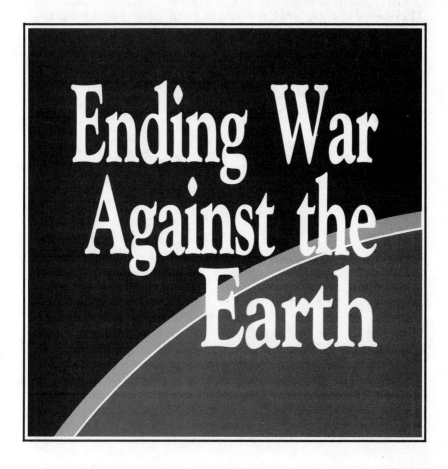

Ending War Against the Earth

Gary E. McCuen

IDEAS IN CONFLICT SERIES

publications inc.

502 Second Street
Hudson, Wisconsin 54016

NUV 1 b 1998

Illustration & Photo Credits

Etta Hulme 10, Joe Heller 15, Locher 21, 34, Blashko 28, 127, Lisa Blackshear 40, US Department of Energy 46, 51, David Seavey 23, 84, 121, Union of Concerned Scientists 91, 95, Carol*Simpson 101, 137, 163, Sack 145, H. Payne 158. Cover illustration by Ron Swanson.

©1991 by Gary E. McCuen Publications, Inc.
502 Second Street, Hudson, Wisconsin 54016
(715) 386-7113

International Standard Book Number 0-86596-081-X Printed in the United States of America

CONTENTS

Ideas in Conflict

CHAPTER 1   GLOBAL CLIMATE CHANGE THROUGH HISTORY: AN OVERVIEW

1. A GEOLOGIC HISTORY OF CLIMATE CHANGE   9
   Dallas L. Peck

2. ECOLOGICAL DEVASTATION AND DECLINING CIVILIZATIONS   13
   Timothy C. Weiskel

3. CLIMATE CHANGE IN THE MODERN ERA   19
   A. Alan Hill

CHAPTER 2   THE EARTH IN CRISIS

4. A PLANET AT RISK   26
   Thomas B. Stoel, Jr.

5. THE GREENHOUSE CLIMATE OF FEAR   32
   Patrick J. Michaels

6. CLIMATE CHANGE THREATENS GLOBAL SURVIVAL   38
   Perspectives From Poor Nations

7. NO EVIDENCE OF A GREENHOUSE EFFECT   44
   Andrew R. Solow

8. OZONE DEPLETION ENDANGERS ALL LIFE   49
   Albert Gore, Jr.

9. NO PROOF YET OF OZONE CRISIS   54
   S. Fred Singer

10. GLOBAL POPULATION GROWTH MUST BE CURBED   58
   Tristram Coffin

11. POPULATION DOOMSAYERS HAVE BEEN WRONG   64
   Julian L. Simon

12. VANISHING FARMLAND: THE POINT   69
   Lester R. Brown

13. VANISHING FARMLAND: 74
    THE COUNTERPOINT
    Warren T. Brookes

CHAPTER 3   ECOLOGY AND HUMAN VALUES

14. GROWTH IS KILLING THE ENVIRONMENT   82
    Murray Bookchin

15. ECONOMIC GROWTH IS THE SOLUTION   89
    Gro Harlem Bruntland

16. THE ENVIRONMENTAL ELITE'S ATTACK   93
    ON FREE ENTERPRISE
    Capital Research Center

17. ACCOUNTING FOR A HEALTHY   99
    ENVIRONMENT
    James Robertson

18. DEEP ECOLOGY AND ECOTERRORISM   105
    THREATEN OUR FUTURE
    Doug Bandow

19. DEEP ECOLOGY: PRESERVING THE   111
    NATURAL ORDER
    Fritjof Capra

CHAPTER 4   GLOBAL CLIMATE AND POOR
                 NATIONS

20. SAVING THE ENVIRONMENT IN POOR   119
    NATIONS
    Richard E. Bissell

21. ENCOURAGING ENVIRONMENTAL   125
    DEVASTATION
    Brent Blackwelder

22. PROMOTING SUSTAINABLE DEVELOPMENT: 131
    A WORLD BANK PERSPECTIVE
    Jeremy Warford and Zeinah Partow

23. ECOLOGY AND DEVELOPMENT: 135
    A PERSPECTIVE FROM THIRD WORLD WOMEN
    Women's Resource Center, Philippines

CHAPTER 5   PUBLIC POLICY AND CLIMATE CHANGE

24. THE POLITICS OF ECOLOGY:
    IDEAS IN CONFLICT
    Howard Hawkins   143

25. WHY WE ARE FAILING   150
    Barry Commoner

26. WHY WE ARE SUCCEEDING   156
    William A. Nitze

27. HUMAN VALUES IN A SUSTAINABLE WORLD   161
    Lester R. Brown, Christopher Flavin and Sandra Postel

28. FREE MARKET VALUES WILL PROTECT   168
    THE ENVIRONMENT
    Fred Smith

Bibliography   173

REASONING SKILL DEVELOPMENT

These activities may be used as individualized study guides for students in libraries and resource centers or as discussion catalysts in small group and classroom discussions.

1. Interpreting Editorial Cartoons   22

2. Examining Counterpoints   78

3. Recognizing Author's Points of View   116

4. What Is Editorial Bias?   140

IDEAS in CONFLICT ®

This series features ideas in conflict on political, social, and moral issues. It presents counterpoints, debates, opinions, commentary, and analysis for use in libraries and classrooms. Each title in the series uses one or more of the following basic elements:

Introductions *that present an issue overview giving historic background and/or a description of the controversy.*

Counterpoints *and debates carefully chosen from publications, books, and position papers on the political right and left to help librarians and teachers respond to requests that treatment of public issues be fair and balanced.*

Symposiums *and forums that go beyond debates that can polarize and oversimplify. These present commentary from across the political spectrum that reflect how complex issues attract many shades of opinion.*

A **global** *emphasis with foreign perspectives and surveys on various moral questions and political issues that will help readers to place subject matter in a less culture-bound and ethnocentric frame of reference. In an ever-shrinking and interdependent world, understanding and cooperation are essential. Many issues are global in nature and can be effectively dealt with only by common efforts and international understanding.*

Reasoning skill *study guides and discussion activities provide ready-made tools for helping with critical reading and evaluation of content. The guides and activities deal with one or more of the following:*

RECOGNIZING AUTHOR'S POINT OF VIEW

INTERPRETING EDITORIAL CARTOONS

VALUES IN CONFLICT

WHAT IS EDITORIAL BIAS?

WHAT IS SEX BIAS?

WHAT IS POLITICAL BIAS?

WHAT IS ETHNOCENTRIC BIAS?

WHAT IS RACE BIAS?

WHAT IS RELIGIOUS BIAS?

*From across **the political spectrum** varied sources are presented for research projects and classroom discussions. Diverse opinions in the series come from magazines, newspapers, syndicated columnists, books, political speeches, foreign nations, and position papers by corporations and nonprofit institutions.*

About the Editor

Gary E. McCuen is an editor and publisher of anthologies for public libraries and curriculum materials for schools. Over the past years his publications have specialized in social, moral and political conflict. They include books, pamphlets, cassettes, tabloids, filmstrips and simulation games, many of them designed from his curriculums during 11 years of teaching junior and senior high school social studies. At present he is the editor and publisher of the *Ideas in Conflict* series and the *Editorial Forum* series.

CHAPTER 1

GLOBAL CLIMATE CHANGE THROUGH HISTORY: AN OVERVIEW

1. A GEOLOGIC HISTORY OF CLIMATE CHANGE 9
   Dallas L. Peck

2. ECOLOGICAL DEVASTATION AND DECLINING CIVILIZATIONS 13
   Timothy C. Weiskel

3. CLIMATE CHANGE IN THE MODERN ERA 19
   A. Alan Hill

1 GLOBAL CLIMATE CHANGE THROUGH HISTORY

A GEOLOGIC HISTORY OF CLIMATE CHANGE

Dallas L. Peck

Natural Variability of Global Climate Occurs on All Time Scales

The geologic record shows that earth's climate has varied substantially in the past, and evidence of past variability of climate can be seen on all time scales. While the causes of climate change are not well understood, we do know that different major influences on global climate operate on various time scales.

A. The Past 140 Million Years:

- Reconstruction of the temperature of deep ocean waters during the past 140 million years (based on oxygen isotope variations preserved in marine fossils) shows that the overall temperature trend over the past 90 million years has been towards colder conditions.

- Superimposed upon the long-term trend toward cooler conditions are significant climatic oscillations on time scales of millions of years, the causes of which are poorly understood.

- The global cooling trend implied by the deep water ocean temperature reconstructions for the past 90 million years cannot be adequately explained by any single mechanism.

B. The Past Two Million Years:

Climate changes that occurred over time intervals of tens of thousands to hundreds of thousands of years have been reconstructed for the past two million years from evidence in sediment cores from the oceans.

Statement of Dallas L. Peck, Director U.S. Geological Survey, Department of the Interior before the Committee on Commerce, Science, and Transportation Subcommittee on Science, Technology, and Space, United States Senate, May 8, 1989.

Variations in oxygen isotopes preserved in marine fossils over thousands of years are plotted as a graph and interpreted as a temperature record. Current evidence suggests that much of the climatic variability observed during the past two million years, on time scales of tens of thousands to about one hundred thousand years, can be explained by celestial mechanics. Systematic variations in the position of earth in its orbit in relationship to the sun, and the changing shape of the orbit over time alters the amount and global distribution of solar energy that strikes the earth. These orbital factors appear to have had a significant influence on the earth's climate.

- Most of the past 2 million years of earth history has been characterized by climates cooler or significantly colder than that of the present day.

- The present global mean annual temperature is about 15 degrees Celsius (59 degrees Fahrenheit). Only a few tens of thousands of years out of the last 2 million years have been characterized by climates as warm as that of the past 10,000 years (the Holocene epoch).

- During the coldest intervals of the first 2 million years, global mean annual temperature dropped about 5 degrees Celsius (9 degrees F).

- During the warmest intervals of the last 2 million years, global temperatures are not likely to have been any warmer than about 2 degrees C (3.6 degrees F) above present day mean annual temperature (15 degrees C).

- A rapid warming for the next century of 2 to 5 degrees C (3.6 to 9 degrees F), which is the general consensus of General Circulation Models (GCM's) when they are run using fossil fuel scenarios to estimate the transient response of the climate system, would be a very unusual event in recent earth history (the past 2 million years or more). If such a rapid warming were to occur, it would be difficult to fully anticipate its consequences. Unfortunately, there is a high degree of uncertainty about the likely rate of warming. . .

C. The Past 11,000 Years:

A simplified temperature curve showing approximate variation in global mean annual temperature spanning the past 11,000 years shows that significant climate changes have occurred on time scales of centuries during that interval. The warming interval 10,500 to about 9,500 years ago was the transition from glacial to "interglacial" climates.

- During the past 10,000 years there have been several intervals when global temperatures were as much as 1.5 to 2 degrees C (2.7 to 3.6 degrees F) warmer than today. None of these previous warming events, which appear to have lasted about 1000 to 1500 years, was caused by human influences on the environment.

- Several intervals of cooler-than-present climate have occurred during the past 10,000 years. The most recent event, called the "Little Ice Age", ended only about 1850 A.D. At least some of the apparent global warming during the last 140 years may be a natural variation, or "recovery"

11

from the Little Ice Age. This complicates the interpretation of possible causal relationships between the apparent global temperature increases of the past century and the observed increases of the past century and the observed increases in carbon dioxide content of the atmosphere during that time.

- The causes of climate oscillations on time scales of decades to millennia during the past 10,000 years are not well understood. Additional research is needed to improve our knowledge of the causes of natural variability of climate on these shorter time scales. . .

Summary

The geologic record contains a valuable source of information about past climate variability on all time scales and can provide important insights into the consequences of climate change. It can tell us how individual species of organisms or entire ecosystems respond to warmer or colder climates and how fast they can respond under natural conditions.

2 GLOBAL CLIMATE CHANGE THROUGH HISTORY

ECOLOGICAL DEVASTATION AND DECLINING CIVILIZATIONS

Timothy C. Weiskel

If we continue to tie our society's infrastructure and agricultural production to a declining resource base—as ancient civilizations did with such depressing regularity—we too will suffer the fate of unavoidable collapse.

Current news on environmental problems frequently emphasizes the totally unprecedented nature of the ecological crisis that besets us in this nation and the western world as a whole. We are told, for example, that the last few months constituted "the hottest summer on record" in North America. Similarly we hear that Boston harbor has never in its history been so polluted, and in European waters seal populations are now dying of an epidemic on a scale never before witnessed by man. By stressing this "never before" aspect of events, it is sometimes argued that the experience of the past is largely irrelevant for policy planners. Since circumstances are so new, so the argument goes, past experience leaves us with little or no instruction in the formulation of a practical public policy for the environment.

Is Our Predicament So New?

This is not altogether true. While particular types of industrial pollution may be new and the scale of ecological devastation may be greater now than previously, recent research demonstrates that the western world is not confronting completely unprecedented circumstances. We need only cast our gaze over a somewhat enlarged horizon to realize that numerous civilizations before our own have confronted environmental degradation.

Excerpted from testimony by Timothy C. Weiskel before the Senate Committee on Environment and Public Works Subcommittee on Hazardous Waste and Toxic Substances, September 14 and 16, 1988. Mr. Weiskel is a professor of Anthropology at Harvard University.

Moreover, many regions of the non-western world are currently facing, and some are coping with, environmental deterioration in our own time.

Historians and archaeologists have studied examples of ecological collapse in past civilizations while anthropologists are examining contemporary examples of ecological degradation in non-western cultures. In our urgent concern to formulate effective environmental policy in the United States, it would be wise to keep the insights of this historical and cross-cultural research clearly in mind, lest public leaders commit our society to repeating and amplifying the tragic blunders of other cultures and past civilizations. If we continue to tie our society's infrastructure and agricultural production to a declining resource base — as ancient civilizations did with such depressing regularity — we too will suffer the fate of unavoidable collapse.

The Ecological Decline of Ancient Civilizations

The record of anthropogenic ecological degradation is, unfortunately, very ancient indeed. Since at least the advent of sedentary agriculture mankind has acted as a powerful biological and geological agent in complex ecosystems, almost invariably without a corresponding awareness of his own impact upon the environment. For this reason, conscious statements by witnesses from the past or from other cultures in our own day have not adequately reflected the full scope of human involvement in ecological decline. Thus, written or oral records are not in themselves sufficient for investigating the question of human agency in ecosystems. Nevertheless, new research techniques have revealed that many catastrophes which have long been understood as "acts of God" or "natural disasters" were, in fact, largely generated or substantially aggravated by collective and cumulative human behavior.

The repeated pattern of the rise and fall of ancient civilizations in the Mediterranean region is especially revealing in this respect. Recent archaeological research indicates that there was a substantial ecological component to the emergence and collapse of agricultural complexes in ancient Mesopotamia, Phoenecia, Palestine, Egypt, Greece and Rome.

These urban-based civilizations had to solve the basic problem of producing food surpluses and collecting raw materials from rural areas to sustain the non-agricultural activities of populations engaged in commerce, ritual, government and the arts. Over time the strategies that each society pursued to produce food and procure resources left their characteristic mark on the environment they inhabited. Some of these strategies proved not to be sustainable in the long run. Local populations either overtaxed the natural resource base of the region (depletion of water, soil, or forest reserves) or the

repeated agricultural demands on the land exceeded its long-term carrying capacity. The general pattern was one of gradual emergence, bringing prosperity, and rapid collapse of civilizations, often taking the form in the final stages of devastating military struggles for the control of arable land or a declining resource base.

Agricultural Use

Techniques of agricultural intensification, — terracing, crop selection, animal husbandry, irrigation, and the like — were devised to meet repeated crises of production. Despite short-term improvements in output, however, the long-term consequences of these technologies were not foreseeable by early agricultural innovators. In subsequent decades or centuries, problems of overgrazing, water-shed deforestation, soil erosion, siltation, water-logging, soil salinization and crop blight often emerged as the long-term consequences of earlier innovations, sometimes leaving whole regions permanently destroyed for agricultural use.

Written documentation concerning these phenomena frequently presents explanations in terms of military, political or religious rivalry and conflict, perhaps most obviously because the elites that wrote such literature were part of military, political or religious institutions in the societies concerned. Nevertheless, no matter how persuasive this literature is, their explanations inevitably oversimplify and distort a more fundamental understanding of the dynamics of agricultural civilizations.

Current archaeological research based upon scientific analysis of soil profiles, vegetation, and landscape evolution indicates that in the rise and fall of ancient civilizations, there was at the base of nearly all sustained conflict an irreducible ecological component. Patterns of rivalry in the Mediterranean could express either a momentary ecological crisis or a long-standing decline of some fundamental element of ecological capital of the agricultural systems concerned. The ecological dislocations were frequently most visible in the "peripheral" areas of the great mediterranean empires, for it was here that the imperial powers established systems of commercial agriculture and proceeded to exact levels of agricultural production that exceeded the ecological capacity of the land. . .

"Development" and Ecological Degradation in the Contemporary Third World

The decline of past civilizations or the violent and explosive characteristics of colonial ecologies might well remain comfortably remote from us in our twentieth century world were it not for the disturbing parallels that such case histories seem to evoke as we consider our contemporary global circumstance. Just as in ancient times and in the age of colonial expansion, it is in the "remote environments," usually quite distant from the centers of power, that the crucial indicators of environmental catastrophe first become apparent within the system as a whole. These regions are frequently characterized by weak economies and highly vulnerable ecosystems in our time, just as they were in the past. Because of these attributes, the environmental circumstances in these regions constitute a kind of monitoring device in the modern world that can provide us with an early warning mechanism for the ecological stability of the global ecosystem as a whole.

If we begin to monitor this early warning system, we will recognize that the signs are not encouraging. One observer has summed up the overall situation quite succinctly:

". . .the last thirty years have been the most disastrous in the history of most, if not all, Third World countries. There has been massive deforestation, soil erosion and desertification. The incidence of floods and droughts has increased dramatically as has their destructiveness; population growth has surged, as has urbanization; in particular, the development of vast shanty-towns, in which human life has attained a degree of squalor probably unprecedented outside Hitler's concentration camps.

Such developments have produced increased malnutrition and hunger; so much so, that today we are witnessing for the first time in human history, famine on a continental scale, with two-thirds of African countries to some degree affected."

While it is most convincing to witness these trends in the field, their reality is apparent to anyone capable of a sensitive reading of available figures and reports that deal with aggregate populations. Several well-documented environmental and economic trends are of particular importance in this connection. These include problems of deforestation, the expansion of petro-chemical agriculture, the shift in weather patterns and perhaps climate in the semi-arid areas, continued population growth and the penetration of local food markets with western food surpluses through dumping or foreign aid.

One of the most familiar among the measured environmental trends in the Third World is the phenomenon of tropical deforestation. While anthropologists have observed this on a micro-ecological basis for several decades, it is now becoming measurable from satellite monitors in space. The scope of the transformation is massive. In March 1984, the Office of Technology Assessment (OTA) reported to the United States Congress that deforestation in tropical areas was proceeding at an alarming rate: "Each year approximately 11.3 million hectares (4.57 million acres) of the earth's remaining tropical forests—an area roughly the size of Pennsylvania—are cleared and converted to other uses," the report indicated. If current trends persist, the report makes it clear that much of the earth's tropical rain forest will be gone by the turn of the century. It estimates that at current the rate, "Nine tropical countries would eliminate practically all of their closed forests within the next 30 years and another 13 countries would exhaust theirs within 55 years."

As scientists are informing us, the tragedies involved in the loss of tropical forests are far greater than the hardships these losses impose on local peasantries or isolated ecologies.

Indeed, the tropical rain forests are perhaps the greatest remaining store of biological diversity left on the planet. Secondly, these ecosystems play a major role in the bio-geo-chemical cycling of carbon and the earth's atmospheric gases. Thirdly, and partly as a result of their role in the bio-geo-chemical cycles, the tropical rain forests appear to play an as yet unclear, but nonetheless, important role in the regulation of the earth's climate.

3 GLOBAL CLIMATE CHANGE THROUGH HISTORY

CLIMATE CHANGE IN THE MODERN ERA

A. Alan Hill

While the phenomenon of stratospheric ozone depletion is a relatively recent discovery, global warming was predicted in 1896 by a Swedish chemist.

Beginning in 1987, the Council on Environmental Quality (CEQ) held a series of public meetings related to stratospheric ozone depletion and global warming. CEQ heard not only from noted scientists on the probable causation of these phenomena, but also from experts on the possible human health, biological, terrestrial, and aquatic effects. . .

While there are many unanswered questions with respect to stratospheric ozone depletion and global warming, the Council recognizes that the available scientific evidence regarding these phenomena furnishes sufficient cause for serious concern. Rather than wait until all scientific uncertainties are resolved, the Council has concluded that federal agencies should begin now to examine how their actions may contribute to, and could be affected by, global climatic change. . .

Stratospheric Ozone Depletion

In 1974, scientists first hypothesized that the use of chlorofluorocarbons (CFCs) could deplete the stratospheric ozone layer. Under this hypothesis, CFCs, emitted at the earth's surface in increasing quantities, slowly diffuse to and degrade in the stratosphere, breaking into chlorine atoms which ultimately chemically destroy ozone molecules. This chemical process results in a thinning of the stratospheric ozone layer.

Statement of A. Alan Hill Chairman, Council on Environmental Quality and Director, Office of Environmental Quality before the Subcommittee on Superfund, Ocean and Water Protection Senate Committee on Environment and Public Works, June 1, 1989.

POVERTY AND POLLUTION

In the developing countries, population growth and pervasive mass poverty continue to undermine the natural resource base which is essential for the success of economic development efforts. Deserts continue to expand and forests to decline. The biological diversity of the planet is diminished. Water pollution threatens the health of millions of people, hindering their capacity to participate productively in economic activities. At the same time, outside international pressures — severe debt burdens, declining commodity prices, protectionist barriers and reduced development assistance — deny developing countries the chance to succeed in their development efforts and to respond effectively to their environmental crises. . .

From a speech by U.S. Secretary-General Javier Perez de Cuellar, September, 1989

A thinner ozone layer would absorb less solar ultraviolet (UV) light and would allow increased UV radiation to reach the earth's surface. Excess amounts of UV radiation are associated with increased incidence of skin cancer, cataracts, and other biological effects such as reduced crop yields and disruption of some terrestrial and aquatic ecosystems.

Research conducted into the response of the stratosphere to ozone-altering compounds and long-term monitoring done to obtain direct evidence of the predicted effect on stratospheric ozone have substantially increased confidence in the ozone depletion hypothesis. For example, there is emerging scientific consensus that the ozone "hole" over Antarctica is due to the reaction of CFCs in the unusually cold Antarctic stratosphere. Most atmospheric scientists do believe that if the present growth rates of CFCs and other ozone-depleting gases continue unabated indefinitely, then it is highly likely that substantial global ozone depletion will occur in the next century, particularly at the higher altitudes and latitudes.

Global Warming

While the phenomenon of stratospheric ozone depletion is a relatively recent discovery, global warming was predicted in 1896 by a Swedish chemist who postulated that the increasing atmospheric concentration of carbon dioxide and other gases from industrialization would trap more solar heat, thus raising the earth's temperature. Scientific research conducted to date has demonstrated that atmospheric levels of carbon dioxide have increased 25% since pre-industrial times and continue to rise.

Reprinted by permission: *Tribune Media Services.*

The National Academy of Sciences has estimated that a doubling of carbon dioxide concentration, which could occur by the middle of the next century, would lead to global warming of 1.5 to 4.5 degrees Celsius (3 to 8 degrees Fahrenheit).

Greenhouse gases include carbon dioxide, methane, and nitrous oxide. These gases occur naturally, but are also produced industrially. For example, the burning of fossil fuels introduces a large amount of carbon dioxide into the atmosphere. Ozone, a pollutant which is chemically produced in the lower atmosphere, and CFCs are still other greenhouse gases.

A warming of the earth's temperature could cause changes in global climatology, such as possible shifts of desert and fertile regions, intensification of tropical storms, and a rise in sea level caused by expansion of sea water as it warms and by glacial melting. Although there are still considerable doubts with respect to the timing and extent of global warming, most scientists consider it highly likely that a global warming trend will eventually be caused by an increased concentration of greenhouse gases. . .

The available scientific evidence and the presentations made in CEQ's public meeting indicate that stratospheric ozone depletion and global warming are "reasonably foreseeable" impacts of emissions of CFCs, halons, and greenhouse gases.

INTERPRETING EDITORIAL CARTOONS

This activity may be used as an individualized study guide for students in libraries and resource centers or as a discussion catalyst in small group and classroom discussions.

Although cartoons are usually humorous, the main intent of most political cartoonists is not to entertain. Cartoons express serious social comment about important issues. Using graphics and visual arts, the cartoonist expresses opinions and attitudes. By employing an entertaining and often light-hearted visual format, cartoonists may have as much or more impact on national and world issues as editorials and syndicated columnists.

Points to Consider

1. Examine the cartoon in this activity. (see next page)

2. How would you describe the message of the cartoon? Try to describe the message in one to three sentences.

3. Do you agree with the message expressed in the cartoon? Why or why not?

4. Does the cartoon support the author's point of view in any of the readings in this publication? If the answer is yes, be specific about which reading or readings and why.

5. Are any of the readings in Chapter One in basic agreement with the cartoon?

Illustration by David Seavey. Copyright 1989, *USA Today*. Reprinted with permission.

CHAPTER 2

THE EARTH IN CRISIS

4. A PLANET AT RISK   26
    Thomas B. Stoel, Jr.

5. THE GREENHOUSE CLIMATE OF FEAR   32
    Patrick J. Michaels

6. CLIMATE CHANGE THREATENS   38
    GLOBAL SURVIVAL
    Perspectives from Poor Nations

7. NO EVIDENCE OF A GREENHOUSE   44
    EFFECT
    Andrew R. Solow

8. OZONE DEPLETION ENDANGERS   49
    ALL LIFE
    Albert Gore, Jr.

9. NO PROOF YET OF OZONE CRISIS   54
    S. Fred Singer

10. GLOBAL POPULATION GROWTH   58
    MUST BE CURBED
    Tristram Coffin

11. POPULATION DOOMSAYERS   64
    HAVE BEEN WRONG
    Julian L. Simon

12. VANISHING FARMLAND: THE POINT   69
     Lester R. Brown

13. VANISHING FARMLAND: 74
     THE COUNTERPOINT
     Warren T. Brookes

4

THE EARTH IN CRISIS

A PLANET AT RISK

Thomas B. Stoel, Jr.

Thomas B. Stoel, Jr., is Director of the International Program at the Natural Resources Defense Council (NRDC). NRDC is one of the nation's leading environmental organizations, with more than 75,000 members in every state and many foreign countries.

Points to Consider:

1. Describe the economic consequences of global warming.

2. How much do scientists think the earth will warm in the next 100 years?

3. What will be the major consequences of global warming?

4. What action should the nations of the world take?

5. What actions should the United States take?

Excerpted from testimony by Thomas B. Stoel, Jr., before the House Foreign Affairs Subcommittee on Human Rights and International Organizations, March 10, 1988.

There is an increasing scientific consensus that the earth is irrevocably committed to a rise in global temperature greater than any in recorded history.

It appears that human activities are altering the climate of the earth at a rate that, if continued, will wreak havoc on the agricultural and natural systems of the planet that support human societies. The attempt to cope with these unprecedented rapid changes could absorb much of the available economic surplus produced by humankind, putting an end to improvements in living conditions. In the face of rapid change in climate and increased climatic instability, global political tensions could be expected to rise precipitously. The likelihood of war and revolution would rise drastically, as climatic instability threatens the economic advantages of wealthy nations and the survival of hundreds of millions in poor countries.

There is an increasing scientific consensus that the earth is irrevocably committed to a rise in global temperature greater than any in recorded history. The National Academy of Sciences has estimated the potential increase in the next 50 to 100 years at between 2.7 and 8.1 degrees Fahrenheit. At the low end of this range, the increase would bring global average temperatures to a level not seen in 6000 years. At the high end, we would have to adjust, within less than a century, to average temperatures not seen since the age of the dinosaurs.

Among the certain consequences of global warming are higher sea levels as oceans expand and polar ice melts; extraordinary changes in weather and rainfall patterns and distributions of forests and plant life; and disruptions in current agricultural patterns. The question in every case is not whether these effects will occur, but how much and how fast. The impacts will be neither smooth nor gradual nor predictable.

Until now, rainfall, climate, and related features such as wetlands have changed over millennia. But the likely consequences of global warming include profound effects on the distribution of arable land, and productivity of agriculture, the distribution of forests, the availability of fresh water in lakes and streams, the productivity of grazing areas and fisheries, all on a time scale measured in decades.

The Consequences Are Mind-Boggling:

- The two-foot rise in sea level, within the range of current predictions, would destroy 80% of U.S. coastal wetlands, inundate 20% of the inhabited land of Egypt, force salt water into coastal drinking water systems, cause massive, sudden and — given coastal storms — violent changes in the economy and usability of shorelines worldwide.

Cartoon by Blashko in *People's Daily World*

- One U.S. Government model predicts a tripling of the number of days above 95 degrees Fahrenheit in the Corn Belt if the average temperature globally rises only a relatively moderate 1.7 degrees C (3 degrees F). At critical points in the growing season, such conditions are certain to reduce yields and would change existing patterns of agriculture.

- The U.S. Corn Belt would not simply move north. Differences in soil suitability and the availability of water, to say nothing of infrastructure, suggest that the agricultural economy would fall seriously out of balance not only in North America but all over the world.

- Global average changes will mask more dramatic regional changes, especially at the middle and higher latitudes, where a 4.5 degree F global average increase might mean a 10 degree increase on a regional basis.

- The eastern United States and the eastern Mediterranean may have had a foretaste of global warming during the summer of 1987. Many areas (including Washington D.C.) experienced the hottest July on record. Urban areas suffered under related pollution episodes that in metropolitan New York exposed the population to smog levels 2.5 times the health-based exposure limit established by the Environmental Protection Agency (EPA). In Greece, the oppressive heat and related smog left at least 700 dead.

Overall Trends

While the extent and consequences of global temperature rise are matters of scientific debate, predictions of the overall trend are not under serious challenge. Nor is the cause. In 1985 the world's leading atmospheric scientists concluded after a meeting in Villach, Austria, that we may experience "in the first half of the next century, a rise in global mean temperature. . .which is greater than any in man's history," and that this increase will be "a result of the increasing concentrations of greenhouse gases [in the atmosphere]."

One of the most respected atmosphere scientists, Dr. Stephen Schneider of the National Center for Atmospheric Research, has said: "The greenhouse theory is the least controversial theory in atmospheric science." NASA scientist Jerry D. Mahlman says "We are virtually certain the climate will warm as these gases increase."

The "greenhouse gases" include carbon dioxide, nitrous oxide, chlorofluorocarbons (CFCs), and methane. All are on the increase in the atmosphere as a result of human activities since the Industrial Revolution. Carbon dioxide and nitrous oxide are emitted by burning fossil fuels; CFCs are artificial compounds used as refrigerants, solvents, foam-blowing agents, and aerosol propellants; increases in methane emission may be related to intensification of agricultural activities to meet the needs of growing populations.

Current emissions of these gases far exceed the ability of forests and oceans to absorb them. Every year, fossil fuel combustion generates five billion tons of carbon emission. Natural mechanisms remove only about half the total. Atmospheric carbon concentrations have increased from their historical level of about 270 parts per million to about 345 parts per million. Atmospheric methane concentrations have more than doubled in the past 300 years, from 680 to 1650 parts per billion, and concentrations have been increasing by more than one percent per year in the past decade.

Despite a U.S. ban on their use as aerosol propellants since 1978, worldwide demand for CFCs is increasing perhaps 3-5% annually. Since the CFCs of greatest concern remain in the atmosphere 75 to 110 years, deep cuts in CFC use, on the order of 85%, would be necessary just to maintain current atmospheric concentrations of CFCs.

Carbon dioxide has often been treated as the only greenhouse gas of significant concern. But, since each greenhouse gas tends to absorb the earth's radiant energy at a different wavelength, the gases work together to block the natural heat loss that keeps the planet's temperature in the moderate, life-sustaining range. Scientists recently have concluded that CO_2 soon will account for about 50% of the warming effect, chlorofluorocarbons 20%, nitrous oxides 7%, methane 12%, and other "trace gases" the remainder. . .

What the World Must Do

There is wide agreement about the actions needed to slow and minimize global warming:

1. *The greatest need is to reduce the rate at which carbon dioxide and nitrous oxide are emitted into the atmosphere.* This can be done by reducing reliance on fossil fuels through greater energy efficiency and increasing use of renewable energy sources.

2. *Global warming also can be slowed by increasing the globe's forested area, or at least reducing the rate of deforestation.* At present, the global area under forest is declining as tropical forests disappear. Development aid agencies like the U.S. Agency for International Development and

the multilateral development banks can play an important role in reversing this trend.

3. *Nations must virtually eliminate the use of CFCs* that are damaging the stratospheric ozone layer and contributing to global warming. The agreement signed by 24 nations in Montreal last September to reduce production of the most commonly used CFCs by 35% in ten years because of their effect in depleting the stratospheric ozone layer is an important first step.

What the United States Must Do

If the world is to take the actions needed to prevent the devastating effects of global warming, the United States must be a leader. We are the most powerful nation in the world, and the leader of the Western industrialized nations which possess most of the world's technical knowledge and economic wealth.

The actions we should take include the following:

1. *Put the issue of global warming on the global political agenda* by calling an international meeting of political leaders to consider what needs to be done.

2. *Encourage the United Nations Environment Program to begin work immediately on a global agreement allocating carbon dioxide emissions among nations.*

3. *Take the lead in reconvening the parties to the Montreal CFC convention* and insist that additional actions be taken to control CFC emissions. Political compromises just aren't good enough when we are violating planetary limits. To show that we mean business, the United States should enact domestic regulations more stringent than those required by the Montreal protocol, including a rapid phaseout of all CFCs which contribute to the greenhouse effect. This will require U.S. industry to develop substitutes which can be used worldwide.

4. *Put the strongest possible emphasis on energy conservation at home and abroad.*

5. *Take steps to slow deforestation and encourage reforestation.* We should increase our bilateral forestry efforts through US Agency for International Development (USAID); encourage appropriate actions by the multilateral development banks and other development aid agencies, using the Tropical Forests Action Plan as a framework; and reexamine our domestic forestry policies.

5 THE EARTH IN CRISIS

A GREENHOUSE CLIMATE OF FEAR

Patrick J. Michaels

Patrick J. Michaels looks at how concern over the greenhouse effect may be clouding our judgment. Michaels, a professor of environment sciences at the University of Virginia, is a member of the executive board of the American Association of State Climatologists.

Points to Consider:

1. Why might Senator Albert Gore of Tennessee think the following article is irresponsible?

2. What do most people think is happening to the global environment?

3. How might Third World Nations be treated unfairly?

4. What scientific contradictions does the author point out? How shoulod we make public policy decisions that deal with the global environment?

Patrick J. Michaels, "The Greenhouse Climate of Fear" *The Washington Post,* January 8, 1989.

Nonetheless, everybody, it appears, believes that the climate we have grown to know and love, D.C. snowstorms included, is coming to an end.

Warning: Senator Albert Gore has determined that the following article on global warming may be irresponsible. "That we face an ecological crisis without any precedent in historic times is no longer a matter of any dispute worthy of recognition," he told *Time* magazine recently. "And those who, for the purpose of maintaining balance in the debate, take the contrarian view that there is significant uncertainty about whether it's real are hurting our ability to respond."

What a strange sentiment. Scientific ideas stand on their own merits, not on the suppression of some facts and exaggeration of others. And Gore's statement is all the more disconcerting given his position on committees that oversee America's efforts in the environmental sciences.

There's no doubt, of course, that the senator's heart is in the right place. No one wants droughts, hurricanes and flooded cities. But attempting to squash one side of a scientific story is a treacherous business that can have only a negative outcome. As historian Thomas Kuhn has noted, major scientific advances tend to occur when a small group of researchers find problems with a widely accepted paradigm.

Moreover, none of us "contrarians" doubt that the greenhouse effect exists. If carbon dioxide and water didn't absorb the long-wave radiation emanating from the earth, we wouldn't be here—the planet would in an ice ball. What we are saying is that the problem is more complicated and ambiguous than it seems, if only because we are putting more into the atmosphere than just CO_2. In fact, of the hundred-odd scientists in the world actively involved in the study of long-term climate data, only one—James Hansen of NASA—has stated publicly that there is a "high degree of cause and effect" between current temperatures and human alteration of the atmosphere.

Apocalypse Now?

Here's what most observers think has happened to date: Northern Hemisphere temperatures rose about 1 degree Fahrenheit during the first 40 years of this century (before the trace-gas alterations were significant), fell for the next 40 years, and rose again in the '80s. How much is the subject of considerable debate. The fact that there has been no net warming since the 1930s is ascribed to the "fly-wheel" effect or thermal lag of the oceans.

Southern Hemisphere temperatures look a lot like what we would expect in Greenhouse World, except that the magnitude

of the rise is about half of what it should be. Interestingly, that's the hemisphere that is 90 percent water. Even some of the greenhouse firebrands in the research community concede that the difference between the hemispheres—which keeps getting larger—casts serious doubt on our understanding of the entire problem.'

Nonetheless, everybody, it appears, believes that the climate we have grown to know and love, D.C. snowstorms included, is coming to an end. And unless we do something about it we will witness a plethora of pestilence that will make biblical Egyptian plagues feel like a walk in the park. Those, incidentally, took place at the end of a relatively warm period, and one that often is cited as the nearest climate civilized man has seen to the one projected for 2020. (The computer-estimated range of average global warming from a doubling of CO_2 is between 5 and 10 degrees Fahrenheit.)

Clearly, we have an issue that truly frightens most everybody (this author included), and that various groups see as an opportunity to save the world in their own image. That is not a situation that promotes objective knowledge. And that's what we desperately need as we begin making policies that, however laudably motivated, could cause real human suffering.

The Third World

Consider, for example, legislation pending in the House (HR 5460) concerning U.S. involvement in the Third World. In order to fight the greenhouse effect, "priority shall be given to programs that enhance access of the poor to low-cost vehicles and efficient carrying devices, including access to credit for the purchase of bicycles, carts, pack animals and similarly affordable non-motorized vehicles." This low-tech fix—favoring water buffalo over Hondas—accords nicely with everyone's favorite panacea: the planting of trees on "marginal land," which just happens to be where a billion of the world's poor live on subsistence agriculture.

Biologist Dan Janzen of the University of Pennsylvania, who holds the Crawfoord prize, the ecologist's equivalent of the Nobel, commented in a recent issue of *Science* that this was yet another example of forcing the poor to pay for the extravagances of the rich. . .

Recent Revelations

Here are a few recent revelations that somehow got lost with the ozone:

- Last June, NASA's Hansen testified to the Senate that "1988 would be the warmest year on record unless there was a remarkable, improbable cooling in the remainder of the year." Even as he spoke, the tropical Pacific was cooling drastically. There's no way he could have known this, because his analysis didn't include temperatures for the sea surface, which covers 70 percent of the earth. On December 7 he recanted, calling the cooling of late 1988 "remarkable," even though a highly respected scientist with the National Oceanic and Atmospheric Administration counts 19 similar events in the last 102 years.

- All summer, the dean of American Climatologists, Jerome Manias at the Scropps Institution of Oceanography, had been saying there's no way one can scientifically defend any statement linking causation of last summer's drought to the greenhouse effect. Then in the December 23rd issue of *Science,* Kevin Trenberth of the National Center for Atmospheric Research and his coauthors convincingly argued that the drought of '88 was caused by warm ocean temperatures in the tropical Pacific, which have since dropped to near record low values.

- Twentieth-century U.S. temperature data, which formed a

part of NASA's congressional testimony last year, hide a drastic warm-measurement bias. NOAA scientist Tom Karl, who arguably knows more about regional climate variation than anyone in the world, has calculated that NASA's record over the United States has warmed up nearly a degree during this century mainly because cities tend to grow up around their weather stations, not because of the greenhouse effect.

If the effect of urbanization ("artificial" warming) on the temperature record averages the same over the rest of the world (and there's no reason to believe it doesn't), then there may have been no global warming to speak of during the last century. Karl's finding surprised none of us who daily toil with the data. But it should be a major shock to those who are using those figures for policy purposes. It is irresponsible to point this out in public?

- Similar problems surround the effect of ozone depletion, ostensibly caused by chlorofluorocarbons, another greenhouse gas. The amount of Ultraviolet-B radiation (the wave-length that causes skin cancer) is presumed to increase with ozone loss. Yet it has actually declined over the United States since meters were first put out in 1974. If everything were equal (it never is — you're older now and thus more likely to be afflicted) you'd find it harder to get skin cancer in 1989 than before the ozone hole was finally noticed.

Surprisingly, the Antarctic ozone depletion was three times less severe this past winter than it was in 1987. No proponents of the anthropo-generated ozone-depletion model and none of the computer simulations expected such a big change. The total concentration may indeed have been in the "natural" range that should occur there most every year.

If many of these findings are news to ordinary citizens, most policy-makers know them all. Yet these findings either aren't being publicized, or they're being ignored as we march down the high road to change. . .

It is on that highly uncertain foundation that we are setting out to make development policy for the Third World. And if you think West Virginia's got problems now, come back after smoking coal becomes illegal. It's hard to understand how we can justify putting the coal miner's daughter on welfare or condemning Kinshasa to Addfare — particularly with forecasts that are mutually inconsistent.

How to Stay Cool

What's a scientist to do? A little more candor for our media stars wouldn't hurt. In fact, most of us lesser being emphasize the limitation of our work every time we get near a reporter. We should also urge science funding agencies to support more work on the temperature histories, even if subsequent findings may derail the policy express and injure the golden goose of Global Change.

What's a policy-maker to do? Some are taking advantage of uncertainty and public hysteria—the politics of fear—in order to promote sweeping actions that can result in major social problems far from our door.

Far preferable is to do something wholly unpopular given the current mood: Make plans, but do nothing that will injure human beings or increase poverty either here or abroad. Our policies should be no more drastic than the scientific conclusions they are based upon. And at present, the problems with the computer models, and the temperature histories are simply too great. Instead, appropriate agencies should be channeling increased resources toward both those areas. Otherwise, we may very well be about to make a policy blunder of literally global proportions.

But what I fear is that all of the recent findings will be ignored. Policy—especially when promoted by very powerful special interests—has an inertia that is very difficult to overcome once the ball starts rolling which it most certainly has. That makes all the hard work, all the science, inconsequential and irrelevant to those who say: Damn the data, full speed ahead!

THE EARTH IN CRISIS

CLIMATE CHANGE THREATENS GLOBAL SURVIVAL

Perspectives from Poor Nations

Nearly 4 billion of the present human population of 5 billion live in developing countries. They need accelerated economic growth but on an ecologically sustainable basis. It is against this background that the participants of the International Conference on "Global Warming and Climate Change: Perspectives from Developing Countries", who met at New Delhi, India, from February 21 to 23, 1989, present the following analysis and recommendations.

Points to Consider:

1. Why is global warming the gravest crisis ever faced by humankind?

2. Describe the three major inter-related problems of global climate change.

3. How are the consequences of climate change for poor nations described?

4. What action should be taken by the rich nations to correct the problem?

Excerpted from a statement by Developing Countries who met at New Delhi, India, from February 21 to 23, 1989.

The industrial countries, being primarily responsible for increased concentration of carbon dioxide and other greenhouse gases in the earth's atmosphere, must take immediate steps to reduce further increases in the level of carbon dioxide emissions.

Global warming is the greatest crisis ever faced collectively by humankind; unlike other earlier crisis, it is global in nature, threatens the very survival of civilization, and promises to throw up only losers over the entire international socio-economic fabric. The reason for such a potential apocalyptic scenario is simple: climatic changes of geological proportions are occurring over timespans as short as a single human lifetime. The World Bank, regional development banks, and other development assistance agencies will need to reappraise their policies in light of the impending global warming. In particular, developing countries will need assistance in the transition phase from traditional fossil fuels to more appropriate energy forms, and in promoting the preservation of forests and reforestation.

Human activities have opened an era of rapid climate changes that, if unchecked, promise an extraordinary reduction in the potential of the earth to support a reasonable quality of life for all. . .

The Nature of the Problem

There are three distinctly different but strongly inter-related parts of the problem: (1) global chemical pollution; (2) the greenhouse effect of these pollutants; (3) the global climate change, resulting from the greenhouse effect induced by the pollutants. Significant scientific progress has been made in understanding and observationally documenting many of these effects. This progress has led to an international consensus among scientists on the significance and the seriousness of the potential global scale warming and the accompanying rise in sea level. The predicted warming rates for the next several decades are unprecedented in terms of climate changes of the last several thousand years.

Global Chemical Pollution

Instrumented observations of the air have demonstrated that:

(1) The concentration of several gases, such as: carbon dioxide; methane; chlorofluorocarbons amongst several others, have increased significantly during the last century and are continuing to increase substantially.

(2) The increases in the pollutants are caused by a variety of human activities including:

- Fossil fuel combustion

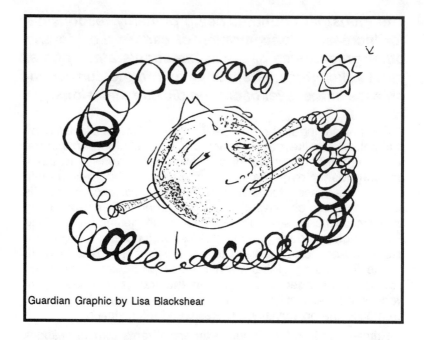

Guardian Graphic by Lisa Blackshear

- Other industrial activities
- Deforestation, biomass burning, and the accelerated decay of organic matter in the soil

(3)   The pollution is global in extent and spreads through the strata of the atmosphere.

The Greenhouse Effect of the Pollutants

(1)   The gases trap the heat radiation from the earth, and hence, the observed rise in the gas concentration has increased the heat trapped in the planet. This so-called greenhouse effect is a well understood phenomenon and is based on sound physical principles.

(2)   Until the 1960s, carbon dioxide increase was the major source of heating. This picture has changed dramatically in the recent decades during which several non-carbon dioxide gases contributed as much as carbon dioxide to the increase in the planetary heating.

(3)   Thus, as time goes by, the problem is getting not only larger in magnitude but more complex in character.

Global Warming and Climate Changes

(1)   The most direct effect of the increased trapping of heat radiation is a global warming.

(2)   The warming will not be globally uniform but will differ significantly between geographical regions; in addition, the warming may vary during different seasons. As a result, the

altered temperature gradients will alter the pattern of winds and precipitation distribution regionally. The details of these localized changes are not clearly understood.

(3) The observed global temperature records, that include ocean and land temperatures, reveal a warming trend during this century; the magnitude of the warming trend is within the range predicted by models. Furthermore, the latter half of the decade of the 1980s registered the warmest temperatures on record.

(4) The warming of the oceans, as well as the melting of ice sheets and glaciers resulting from the warming of the land will lead to a rise in the sea-level. . .

Potential Impact

Global warming is occurring at a time when many of the world's life-support systems are already stressed by the growth of population, industrial development and need for agricultural land and the unsustainable exploitation of natural resources. These stresses are caused both by careless and short-sighted actions and as a consequence of poverty and underdevelopment. They include the increasing air and water pollution, deforestation, soil erosion and salination, among others.

On all of these changes, global warming and associated climate change will bring additional consequences, such as:

- higher temperatures
- changes in precipitation and storm activity
- widespread run-off
- reduction in fresh water availability
- global rising of mean sea level

Effects of sea-level rise include:

- loss of land and human habitation
- penetration of salt into drinking and agricultural water supplies
- beach erosion
- loss of wetland and wildlife habitat, including air fauna
- damage of infrastructure including harbors, cooling water facilities, coastal defense systems, roads and other infrastructure

Ecosystem

Sea-level rise will devastate coastal ecosystems such as mangrove seaways, which no longer migrate inland because of human habitation near the coast.

Terrestrial ecosystems will need to move poleward in response to the warming. However, the rate of warming may exceed the ability of ecosystems to migrate, (or corridors of migration may not be available); so loss of species or reduction in numbers can be expected. In particular, canopy forests may suffer substantial declines.

Loss of carbon from forests and soils due to increased respiration and reduced biomass would add substantially to the build up of CO_2 and thus to the rate of warming.

Perspectives from Developing Countries and Agenda for Action

It is the perception of the participants of the conference that the industrial countries, being primarily responsible for increased concentration of carbon dioxide and other greenhouse gases in the earth's atmosphere, must take immediate steps to reduce further increases in the level of carbon dioxide emissions.

In order to promote energy efficiency and alternative energy sources, fees or taxes must be imposed by the developed countries on the emission of greenhouse gases from fossil fuel use. In this respect, several developing countries have followed very heavy taxation measures, resulting in high prices of petroleum products in particular. This contrasts with the short-sighted decline, particularly in gasoline prices in several western countries, which would only bring about larger increases in private transport, an expanding fleet of gas-guzzling automobiles and a slowing down of public transportation developments. This situation must be reversed through a determined implementation of a new fossil fuel tax regime.

The proposed tax on greenhouse gas emissions should provide finances for measures that can protect global climate. Such funds should be used for:

1) Large scale research, development and demonstration activities related to renewable energy technologies;

2) Transfer of energy efficient technologies from the developed to the developing countries;

3) Financing of forestry and other projects in parts of the world where availability of large scale deforestation calls for immediate measures.

The developing countries must evaluate a range of public policy options that may contribute toward the global effort in countering the greenhouse effect. Unfortunately, not enough research and analysis has been carried out on the economic costs and benefits of the options available, and actions will have to be preceded by adequate analysis in the immediate future.

THE EARTH IN CRISIS

NO EVIDENCE OF A GREENHOUSE EFFECT

Andrew R. Solow

Andrew R. Solow is a statistician at the Woods Hole Oceanographic Institution. He is a member of the Climate Trends Panel established by the National Climate Program Office (NCPO) and also a member of the scientific working group of the Intergovernmental Panel on Climate Change (IPCC) established by the United Nations Environmental Program (UNEP) and the World Meteorological Organization (WMO). His work in the area of climate change has focused on the analysis of climate data, with particular attention to the question of detecting the onset of climate change.

Points to Consider:

1. How is the greenhouse effect process defined?

2. Describe the accuracy and extent of climate data.

3. What does the climate data say about the notion that an "enhanced greenhouse effect" has begun?

4. How much have global temperatures warmed since 1880?

5. How much have temperatures warmed in the United States in the last 100 years?

6. What actions should nations take in regard to global warming?

Excerpted from testimony by Andrew R. Solow before the House Merchant Marine and Fisheries Subcommittee on Oceanography and the Great Lakes, May 4, 1989.

From an objective point of view, there is no compelling evidence that an enhanced greenhouse effect has begun.

The greenhouse effect refers to the process by which trace gases, like carbon dioxide, trap reflected long-wave solar radiation and warm the atmosphere. This connection between atmospheric composition and climate has been known since the last century. The possibility that human activity could alter atmospheric composition enough to enhance the natural greenhouse effect and cause climate change has been recognized for at least fifty years. The level of carbon dioxide in the atmosphere has increased by about 15% since monitoring began thirty years ago, and by about 25% since the beginning of the Industrial Revolution. This increase appears to be due in large part to human activities like the consumption of fossil fuels and large-scale deforestation. In addition to carbon dioxide, a number of other trace gases—including chlorofluorocarbons and methane—have also been identified as greenhouse gases. Their levels also appear to be rising. The connection between atmospheric composition and climate, and the documented changes in atmospheric composition, have led to concern about the possibility of significant global warming and its possible consequences.

It is clear that the appropriate human response to the possibility of climate change depends on many factors including the timing, nature, and magnitude of the change, as well as the benefits and costs of the response itself. A response that would be efficient under a rapid change of large magnitude could be a costly mistake under a slow change of more modest magnitude. Unfortunately, there is a great deal of uncertainty about future climate. This uncertainty complicates the discussion of climate change in general and the choice of policy response in particular. . .

Climate Data

There is a great deal of climate data and a great deal to say about it. One important problem is that many of the records contain a highly localized warming component due to population growth. This is called the urban heat island effect, although there is some evidence that it is present in towns with populations as small as a few thousand. The urban heat island effect may account for up to one-third of the apparent warming since 1880.

Perhaps the most careful regional study of long-term temperature data was that performed by Hanson, Maul, and Karl for the United States. That study showed that there has been no net warming in the United States over the past 100 years.

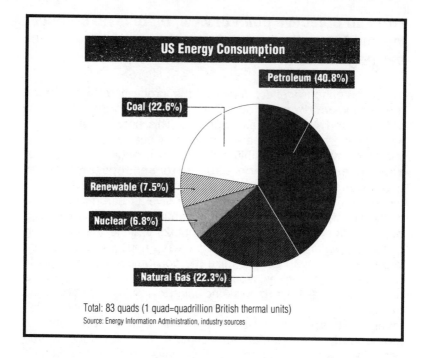

US Energy Consumption

Petroleum (40.8%)

Coal (22.6%)

Renewable (7.5%)

Nuclear (6.8%)

Natural Gas (22.3%)

Total: 83 quads (1 quad=quadrillion British thermal units)
Source: Energy Information Administration, industry sources

To my knowledge, this result has not been challenged in the scientific literature. Some scientists have pointed out quite correctly that the United States covers only a small fraction of the earth's surface, and that it is dangerous to draw too general a conclusion from these results. On the other hand, as a statistician I find it remarkable that, in the only large area for which enough reliable data may be on hand to support such a careful study, there is no evidence of long-term warming.

Despite these reservations, most climatologists believe that there has been some global warming since 1880. The question naturally arises as to whether this warming is related to a human enhancement of the greenhouse effect. For a number of reasons, the answer to this question is probably no.

First, the warming began before an enhanced greenhouse effect could reasonably be expected to have begun. If an enhanced greenhouse effect had begun or intensified during the course of the data, then there should be a systematic acceleration in the rate of warming. No such acceleration appears in the data.

Second, the rate of warming is less than half the rate expected under an enhanced greenhouse effect, even in its early stages.

Third, the spatial distribution of the warming is inconsistent with that expected under an enhanced greenhouse effect. For example, the United States is expected to experience significant warming under an enhanced greenhouse effect. The results of

Hanson, Maul, and Karl show that no such warming has occurred.

Fourth, there is an alternative explanation for the slow apparent warming over the past century. From around 1200 AD to the middle of the 19th century, the earth experienced a cool period known as the Little Ice Age. There is clear evidence of the Little Ice Age in many long-term climatological records. The slow warming over the past 100 years may simply represent a recovery from such a cool event.

Climate is constantly changing. We know that climate can change for reasons other than an enhanced greenhouse effect caused by human activities. Even assuming that the apparent slow, irregular warming that has occurred since 1880 is real, there is no evidence that any of it is due to an enhanced greenhouse effect. In any case, the warming during the 1980s is not strikingly different from warming that occurred earlier in the record. From an objective point of view, there is no compelling evidence that an enhanced greenhouse effect has begun.

Policy, Uncertainty, and Information

I would like to make a few comments about the problem of making policy in the face of uncertainty. . .

It is certainly possible, and probably desirable, to incorporate a preference for caution into the policy process. In general, however, this is not the same thing as assuming that the worst possible situation is sure to occur, even if it has a very small probability of occurring. It is important to realize that there are a number of potential problems facing us with consequences at least as great as climate change. In facing these problems, we do not act as if the worst possible situation is sure to occur, nor should we act this way in facing the problem of climate change.

Large-scale policies aimed at sharply and rapidly curtailing the human activities that contribute carbon dioxide to the atmosphere are certain to be expensive. After all, these activities are not pursued with the sole purpose of changing atmospheric composition. Although it would certainly be a mistake to expand these activities recklessly, given the current uncertainties about climate change, I do not believe that such policies are justified by fears of climate change alone. On the other hand, more modest policies may be appropriate, particularly if they are justified for other reasons as well.

Because the antidote to uncertainty is information, and because information takes time to gather, the proper course of action in some situations is to postpone an active policy response while more information is gathered. In the case of climate change, I believe that the value of information is very great, and that postponing an active response even by several years is very unlikely to have a serious impact on the ultimate outcome of climate change. Of course, some of this research should focus on the design of policies that could be put into place fairly rapidly should further information point to the likelihood of rapid, costly climate change.

Conclusion

There are legitimate reasons for concern over the possibility of significant and costly climate change. In order to respond effectively to climate change, it is necessary to know rather more than that the possibility exists. Unfortunately, substantial uncertainties exist about the timing, nature, and magnitude of climate change. Climate models provide only a crude representation of climate. They do not perform well at reproducing the recent behavior of climate, nor do their forecasts of future climate agree. Climate data do not provide any compelling evidence of the onset of an enhanced greenhouse effect.

The proper way to account for uncertainty in formulating a policy response is not to act as if the worst possible situation is sure to happen. Instead, a balance should be struck between potential benefits, potential costs, and the probabilities of different outcomes. Given the uncertainties about future climate, a large-scale policy response is not justified by fears of climate change alone. The best way to resolve uncertainty is to gather information. With regard to the climate change issue, the value of information is very great and the risks involved in postponing an active policy response are small.

While some see a danger in expressing even legitimate doubts about the possibility of catastrophic climate change, there is also a danger in the way in which the recent discussion has evolved. By acting as if catastrophic climate change is lurking around the corner, and by association in the public's eye certain short-term meteorological events with long-term climate change, we run the risk of losing the public's attention and confidence should dramatic climate change not begin very soon or should other kinds of meteorological events—like a cool, rainy summer— occur.

8   THE EARTH IN CRISIS

OZONE DEPLETION ENDANGERS ALL LIFE

Albert Gore, Jr.

Albert Gore, Jr., is a democratic senator from Tennessee. He is chairman of the Subcommittee on Science, Technology and Space and a leading national advocate for environmental concerns.

Points to Consider:

1. Why is depletion of stratospheric ozone a pressing concern?

2. How does ozone protect the planet?

3. Identify the extent of global ozone depletion.

4. What are CFCs and why should they be banned from production?

Excerpted from a statement by Senator Albert Gore, Jr., before the Subcommittee on Science, Technology and Space of the Senate Committee on Commerce, Science and Transportation, February 23, 1989.

The scientists tell us there must be at least an 85 percent reduction just to stabilize the rate of damage, not to reduce the rate of damage, but just to stabilize the rate of damage.

I want to particularly welcome the scientists on the first panel from the National Aeronautics and Space Administration and the National Oceanic and Atmospheric Administration, because they have just returned from a history-making expedition to the Arctic and their work will, of necessity, be reflected in our policy and in our very way of life. I also want to welcome our witnesses on the second panel from business and industry who are on the front lines of this real world battle.

The scientists on our first panel have used the most complicated instruments and the most sophisticated measuring devices to examine a complex threat that has been for many Americans something that somebody else should worry about.

For most families, understandably, the depletion of stratospheric ozone is not nearly as pressing a concern as the mortgage payment. So maybe it is not surprising that when these scientists returned from the Arctic, the first question they faced at a news conference where they discussed their findings was from a journalist looking for explanations in plain language. She was speaking for a large portion of the public.

Activism Needed

Yet as they made clear in that conference, and as I hope will be made even more clear here today, there are compelling reasons to turn this prevailing disinterest into activism. For example, there are now clear warnings of severe economic and social disruptions in the coming decade, the 1990s, unless we move now to reverse the deterioration of our environment.

Ozone depletion is one of the key factors in those warnings. Destruction of the earth's protective ozone shield in the upper atmosphere will mean, according to the scientists, lost protection from the sun's most damaging ultraviolet rays and an increase in skin cancers and cataracts.

Estimates are that for every one percent depletion of the ozone layer, and there have been several percent depleted already, there will be a two percent increase in the incidence of skin cancer. World-wide some 100,000 people each year die from the deadliest forms of skin cancer, and of course millions of others contract the less deadly forms.

Since 1969 in the U.S. alone, ozone concentrations above the continental United States have decreased two to three percent, some argue somewhat more. The mathematics, then, are obviously quite deadly.

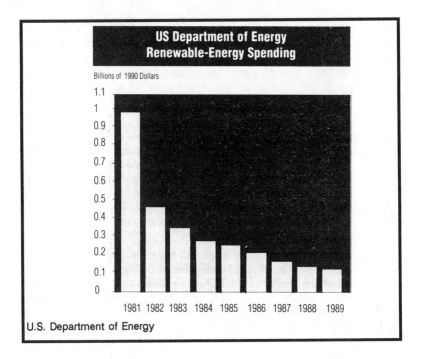

**US Department of Energy
Renewable-Energy Spending**

Billions of 1990 Dollars

U.S. Department of Energy

What may be much worse is that destruction of the earth's protective ozone shield threatens damage farther down the food chain and threatens thousands of plants and crops in ways that scientists have not yet fully measured. It already has resulted in damage to some of the most basic organisms at the bottom of the food chain, the phytoplankton, or the simple sea vegetation in the oceans of the world, particularly in the southern ocean—vegetation that sustains the smallest fish to the largest whale.

Scientists tell us that this problem exists now. The seasonal ozone hole in the upper atmosphere above Antarctica reaches the size of the continental United States. Moreover, conditions at the Arctic, as we will hear today, present a time bomb that could cause similar problems and worse.

CFCs

We know what is punching these holes in the ozone layer: a family of chemicals called chlorofluorocarbons. We put them up there with aerosol sprays, automobile air conditioners, styrofoam and other products. The sad truth is that most of the CFCs we have dumped into our environment have not even reached the upper atmosphere yet.

As a result, between today and the year 2000, the quantity of these chemicals in our upper atmosphere will have doubled. If we think we have a problem now, ten years from now we will have a much bigger problem, because as these scientists will tell us, in the Arctic and Antarctic, the amount of damage done by these chemicals increases by the square of their concentrations.

In other words, as they increased by a factor of 2, the damage increased by a factor of 4. Stated as simply as possible, this is one of the most serious environmental threats that our planet has ever faced, and of course as is by now well known, the very same chemicals that are responsible for virtually all of the destruction of the ozone layer are also responsible for up to 20 percent of the greenhouse effect, or the global warming problem.

Importantly, it is a challenge that we can meet. It may well mean changes in the design of our refrigerators and automobile air conditioners and other products. It may mean we can no longer go to the store and buy freon off the shelf. But as the respected journal *Science* recently stated, that is a small price to pay when one considers the alternative; the loss of the global ozone layer and the resulting havoc wreaked upon much of the life on earth.

We know that reducing our emissions of these chemicals by recapture, recycling and eventual replacement will reduce the environmental risk. . .

Montreal Protocol

There must be a marriage between the scientists and the policymakers. That is the idea behind legislation that I recently introduced as S. 201, which would among other things mandate a rapid phaseout, a complete phaseout of CFCs. I do not believe we can wait any longer to address this problem.

The Montreal Protocol, which the Senate ratified last year, put in place international limits on CFC production. But an effective 35 percent reduction by the end of this century, as the protocol requires, is far too little, far too late. The scientists tell us there must be at least 85 percent reduction just to stabilize the rate of damage, not to reduce the rate of damage but just to stabilize the rate of damage.

So the scientists who have come here today represent our

first defense against global environmental threats like the one we are discussing in this hearing. Recognizing what is happening to our planet will show us what measures we must take to halt the damage. We need a broad international effort to monitor and understand the earth so that we can respond wisely to the global environmental crises, from ozone depletion and global warming to deforestation and acid rain.

THE EARTH IN CRISIS

NO PROOF YET OF OZONE CRISIS

S. Fred Singer

S. Fred Singer, Professor of Environmental Sciences at the University of Virginia, finds that ozone in the earth's atmosphere which protects man from harmful ultraviolet radiation, is not at an abnormally low level. Seasonal declines in ozone over Antarctica have been observed for over 30 years and have had no adverse effects on living creatures.

Points to Consider:

1. How is ozone on the planet's surface different from ozone in the stratosphere?

2. What are CFCs and how are they accused of damaging the environment?

3. How serious is the ozone depletion in Antarctica?

4. Why would elimination of CFCs be a mistake?

S. Fred Singer, "Stratosphere Ozone", Heritage Paper Backgrounder for Earth Day, April 19, 1990.

The case against CFCs is based on the scientific theory of ozone depletion, plausible but quite incomplete—and certainly not reliable in its quantitative predictions.

Ozone is a natural component of the earth's atmosphere. It is a type of oxygen molecule formed when high energy components of solar radiation break apart other compounds, allowing the oxygen to recombine as ozone. In high concentrations at the planet's surface, ozone is considered a pollutant that can irritate lungs and eyes, and lower crop yields. This ozone can be created by reactions of either manmade or natural chemicals and is a primary constituent of urban "smog".

High in the stratosphere, however, ozone forms a natural layer that efficiently absorbs ultraviolet (UV) radiation from the sun. UV radiation is the tanning component of sunlight, and has been linked to benign, non-melanoma skin cancers. UV radiation also can stimulate the body to produce Vitamin D, which can reduce the incidence of certain diseases, such as rickets and osteoporosis.

Cloud of Suspicion

Some research in the 1970s suggested that the normally inactive chlorofluorocarbons, or CFCs, used in many modern applications, including refrigeration, computer chip manufacture, and fire extinguishers, could percolate up into the stratosphere and there be decomposed and attack ozone. In 1980, the National Academy of Sciences estimated that the maximum possible reduction in stratospheric ozone due to CFCs was approximately 18 percent. Over the years, this number has been revised sharply downward, to as low as between 2 and 4 percent. But the initial estimate has held the public's attention. Under this cloud of suspicion, voluntary restraints on CFC use were adopted for some noncritical applications. By 1978, the U.S. had unilaterally banned CFC use in all aerosol propellants.

In 1985, a British group at an ozone observing station at Halley Bay, Antarctica, announced that every October since 1975 they had found a short-lived decline in the amount of stratospheric ozone. The magnitude of the decrease had grown steadily, reaching nearly 50 percent of the total ozone. The finding was quickly confirmed by satellite instruments, which also indicate that the phenomenon covered a large geographic region. It seemed that a "smoking gun" had been found; linking ozone destruction with CFCs and chlorine, a chemical component of CFCs.

Limited Conditions

However, the precipitous decline observed in ozone levels around October is dependent upon the existence of a number of precise climatic conditions. For example, the stratospheric layers must be isolated from other air layers so that warmer air or chemical "contaminants" do not interfere with the ozone-depleting reaction. These conditions are limited to the South Pole and smaller pockets near the North Pole and even then only for short periods each year.

Further, G.M.B. Dobson, the Oxford University professor who started modern ozone observations, and for whom the measuring unit for ozone is now named, noted this temporary disappearance of ozone in 1956. Dobson noted that when the Halley Bar Antarctic station was first set up in 1956, the monthly reports showed that "the values in September and October 1956 were about 150 [Dobson] units [50 percent] lower than expected. . . .In November the ozone values suddenly jumped up to those expected. . .It was not until a year later, when the same type of annual variation was repeated, that we realized that the early results were indeed correct and that Halley Bay showed a most interesting difference from other parts of the world."

Tremendous Fluctuations

The discovery, or perhaps rediscovery, of the Antarctic ozone "hole" was combined with a March 1988 report by the National Aeronautics and Space Administration Ozone Trends Panel calling for a complete ban on CFCs. The NASA report indicated that global ozone levels had declined by a total of around 3 percent since 1969. This ominous report convinced many that CFCs were destroying ozone throughout the stratosphere. However, the report failed to mention that the year selected as the starting point for ozone measurements was actually a peak year for ozone levels. Since ozone's existence in the stratosphere is closely linked to the amount of solar radiation, it fluctuates tremendously over seasons and from year to year. Additionally, measurements of UV radiation at the earth's surface show that it actually has declined since 1974, even though theory predicts that it should increase when ozone is reduced.

Scientific caution was not followed by many in the international environmental community. Arising from the recommendations of the Montreal Protocol of 1987, drawn up by representatives of most of the world's industrialized countries, global controls for CFCs have been adopted by most of the major industrial nations, calling for a 50 percent reduction in world CFC output by the year 2000. Further demands are being pressed for total elimination of CFCs by the year 2000.

The case against CFCs is based on the scientific theory of

ozone depletion, plausible but quite incomplete—and certainly not reliable in its quantitative predictions. There is even evidence that volcanoes, and perhaps salt spray and bio-chemical emissions from the oceans, contribute substantially to stratospheric amounts of chlorine, which minimizes the effects of manmade CFCs.

Even assuming the accuracy of the current theories, the actual threat would be quite small to both humans and plant and animal life. Normally, UV radiation increases the closer to the equator, or the higher in altitude one goes. A 5 percent decrease in the ozone layer would, under the environmentalist's own theory, increase UV exposure to the same extent as moving about 60 miles south, the distance from Palm Beach to Miami.

Unnecessary Sacrifice

CFCs contribute greatly to the welfare of modern man. They are non-toxic, nonflammable, inexpensive compounds. Alternatives may turn out to be toxic to humans, corrosive to existing equipment, less energy-efficient in use, may decay over time requiring frequent replacement, and are certain to be more costly. With such important and direct consequences resulting from a ban, the scientific supports for a total ban need to be greatly enhanced. Otherwise society will be asked to sacrifice both public health and economic vitality for a threat that may not exist.

THE EARTH IN CRISIS

GLOBAL POPULATION GROWTH MUST BE CURBED

Tristram Coffin

Tristram Coffin is the editor of the Washington Spectator, *a semi-monthly publication of the Public Concern Foundation.*

Points to Consider:

1. How many people will live on the earth by the year 2050?

2. What is the current global population?

3. Describe the special problems of Africa.

4. Identify the social conditions that cause high birthrates in many nations.

5. How successful has irrigation been in helping to feed people?

6. What methods of birth control are used by many governments around the globe?

Tristram Coffin, "Looking Ahead: More Mouths, Less Food". *The Washington Spectator,* May 15, 1990.

The current world population of 5.2 billion will increase this decade by nearly one billion, the fastest population growth in history.

The world's farmers are finding it more difficult to keep up with growth in population.

This modest statement in *State of the World 1990*, by Worldwatch Institute, is an omen of tragedy.

The International Foundation for the Survival and Development of humanity reports: "The uncontrolled growth of the world's population, projected to reach at least 10 billion people by 2050, exacerbates the full range of environmental problems; it increases pressure on forests, water, soils and fisheries; increases the use of nonrenewable resources and the generation of waste; favors the adoption of technologies of production that can increase output in the short term without regard to their environmental costs; and strains the capacity of institutions to plan and manage. The shortage of arable land for food production, insufficient supplies of energy and the spread of malnutrition and disease will worsen as population increases."

These facts are well known to presidents, prime ministers and other political leaders. But they tend to look the other way because the answers often are unpopular.

State of the World describes what is happening today in Africa, where "the combination of record population growth and widespread land degradation is reducing grain production per person. A drop of 20 percent from the peak in 1967 has converted the continent into a grain importer, fueled the region's mounting external debt, and left millions of Africans hungry and physically weakened, drained of their vitality and productivity." What is happening in Africa is "a nightmare scenario," according to the World Bank.

To add to Africa's troubles, the giant desert is spreading ever southward because trees are being cut for firewood.

The current world population of 5.2 billion "will increase this decade by nearly one billion, the fastest population growth in history, threatening to erase the gains that many countries have struggled to achieve," according to a UN report in the *Los Angeles Times.* "In 1990 alone, 90 million to 100 million people, or about the combined population of the Philippines and South Korea, will be added to the world. The decade's growth of one billion will add the equivalent of an extra China to the world's population. . . .By and large, the biggest increase will happen in the poorest countries, those by definition least equipped to meet the needs of the new arrivals and invest in their future."

A Few Answers

The experts suggest four steps to avert serious famine and suffering in this decade:

- Address and change conditions that bring on high birthrates. Worldwatch Institute says that "social [and economic] conditions underlying high fertility" include "the low status of women, illiteracy and low wages."

The Institute for Food and Development Policy points out: "Living at the economic margin, many poor parents perceive their children's labor as necessary to augment meager family income. By working in the fields and around the home, children also free up adults and older siblings to earn outside income."

On the island of Java, children care for chickens and ducks at seven years old, tend goats and cattle at nine, and are sent out to work for wages at 12. In parts of India, 12-year-old girls work up to 10 hours a day picking tea. In Manila, children collect and sell scrap from dumps. "Bangkok and Sao Paulo are both notorious for child prostitutes, many of whom are the sole support of their families."

Many governments and even population-control groups "appear unwilling to address the roots of these problems that lie largely in the economic and political order." Radical reforms inevitably bring tough opposition from those who cling to the status quo. President Francois Mitterand, of France, is one political leader demanding reform. He told the *National Geographic:* "There is madness in not striving to reduce the gap between rich and poor. The gap is more dangerous than nuclear bombs. When people do not have enough to eat—and this will soon be the case in eight out of ten human beings—their revolt can prove impossible to check."

- Boost the status of women in the Third World, so that they will have more control over the number of children they bear. *Population Briefing Paper* reports: "The world's poorest women are not merely poor, they live on the edge of subsistence. They are economically dependent and vulnerable, politically and legally powerless. As wives and mothers, they are caught in a life cycle that begins with an early marriage and too often ends with death in childbirth. They work longer hours and sometimes work harder than men, but their work is typically unpaid and undervalued."

A doctor in a Mexican clinic reports that many women want to avoid or delay pregnancy. "When a wife wants to [try] to limit the number of mouths to feed in the family, the husband will become angry and even beat her. He thinks it is unacceptable that she is making a decision of her own. She is challenging his authority, his power over her—and thus the very nature of his virility." (*Message from the Village,* by Perdita

POPULATION AND RESOURCES

Every minute the global population grows by 150 and every year by 80 million. 93 percent of this growth occurs in developing countries. By 2000, world population will be at 6.1 billion. Half the world will be living in urban areas and one-fifth of these people will be living in mega-cities of 4 million or more.

Only 4 billion of the world's 13.25 billion hectares of land are cultivable. The developing countries have half the cultivated land but contain over three-fourths of the world's population. Over the next 50 years, to meet projected population increases, arable land will have to double as will yield.

Although the industrialized countries contain less than 25 percent of the world's population, they consume 75 percent of the energy used, 79 percent of all commercial fuels, 85 percent of all wood production and 72 percent of all steel production. Overall, they consume about 80 percent of the world's goods, which leaves three-fourths of the population with less than one-fourth of the world's wealth.

From Congressional Testimony by Bruce Halliday, Member of Parliament, House of Commons, Canada, March 2, 1989

Huston)

In many Third World areas, girls marry early: the average age of marriage is 11.6 years in Bangladesh; 15.3 in Pakistan and 15.7 in Sierra Leone. An Indian parent says, "Society will condemn us if our daughters are not married by the age of 15."

- Undertake a program to teach families about birth control. Make it "part of a package which includes other types of investments in human resources," a UN official suggests.

- Provide women with birth control devices and methods. Women are more likely than men to practice birth control.

Use of the Pill

The birth control pill has been particularly popular in the U.S. In an article in *Science,* chemist Carl Djerassi points out: "By the end of the decade [the '60s], the cumulative decision of nearly 10 million American women had made the pill the most popular method of birth control [because of] the privacy it offered a woman."

Use of the pill has decreased recently because of fears of side effects. However, "the consensus now is that for healthy young women, the pill is the most effective contraceptive method and probably one of the safest. Women in their middle thirties or older were thought to be at increased risk in terms of cardiovascular complication, [but] the most recent. . .evidence concerning low-dose pills suggests that such risk applies only to heavy smokers."

In other parts of the world, the IUD is widely used. "In China, at least 35 million women are estimated to be wearing an IUD developed in the 1960s, thus making it the most prevalent contraceptive in that country." *(Science)*

Still another birth control option is RU486, the French pill, that World Development Forum says has been "tested and recognized as a safe, effective and simple means of terminating early pregnancy." The pill works by blocking the normal action of progesterone, thus preventing the fertilized egg from attaching itself to the uterine wall.

The world is teeming with ideas for holding down the birthrate, but in the meantime, food and water supplies in some areas are being critically diminished by the rise in population.

A Look at Irrigation

Irrigation has been a major factor in our ability to feed new millions in this century. One-third of the world's global harvest comes from the 17 percent of cropland that is irrigated. Each year, 3,300 cubic kilometers of water—six times the flow of the Mississippi River—are taken from rivers, streams and underground aquifers.

Yet irrigation is not a total blessing. In dry areas, evaporation of water near the surface leaves a residue of salt that harms crops and may make the land unusable for farming. *State of the World 1990* reports, "Aerial views of abandoned irrigated areas in the world's dry regions reveal vast expanses of glistening white salt, land so destroyed that it is essentially useless." In India, for example, salinity has cut yields on 20 million hectares, and another seven million hectares have been abandoned.

In the ancient past, two great irrigation projects, the "fertile crescent" of the Tigris-Euphrates River and that of the Hohokam Indians in what is now Arizona, were fouled by salinity, according to Robert Kerr, author of *Land, Wood and Water* (Fleet). He points out: "The sun, as it draws water upward in the process of evaporation, leaves salt. Unless the salt accumulation is periodically flushed out of the canals, it will seep into the soil and destroy its fertiliy."

Other problems: water leaking from canals and the over-sprinkling of fields can waterlog the earth and rob plants of oxygen. Also, pumping water to provide irrigation for crops has seriously reduced underground water supplies. In the U.S., water is being pumped into more than four million hectares—about a fifth of the irrigated area—in excess of recharge. In Texas, some water tables have been dropping as much as six inches a year. In north China, a vital wheat-growing area, ground water levels are falling by a meter a year. In Egypt, where almost all cropland is irrigated, half has become salinized, and yields are diminished.

11 THE EARTH IN CRISIS

POPULATION DOOMSAYERS HAVE BEEN WRONG

Julian L. Simon

Julian L. Simon is a Professor of Business Administration at the University of Maryland in College Park. He is a prominent conservative spokesman advocating conservative social and political ideas.

Points to Consider:

1. How have the theories of "population doomsayers" been disproved?

2. What is the relationship between population growth and economic prosperity?

3. Why is the rapid growth of world population a "victory over death"?

4. What is the relationship between population growth and the world environment?

Julian L. Simon, "Statement on Population Growth and Human Welfare", May, 1990. This essay was part of an Earth Day Alternative packet distributed by the Competitive Enterprise Institute in Washington, D.C.

The increase in the world's population represents our victory over death.

The theories of the population doomsayers, which have now been discredited by a solid body of scientific research, have cost the lives of tens of millions, or even hundreds of millions, of human beings in the last decade or so—far more human lives than were lost in World War II.

Yet public fears, and the clamor to reduce population growth and avert more human lives, are back again.

Twenty years ago doomsaying statements about population growth had not yet been disproved. Paul Ehrlich and company could base their assertions upon their raw intuitions coupled with primitive Malthusian reasoning, without fear of being contradicted by solid evidence. . .

Disproved Ideas

By *ten* years ago, science had already disproved the anti-population ideas. These ideas were still an unusual minority position, and it was not unreasonable for you to be skeptical. The research results which had already begun to accumulate could still be ignored as "controversial" by the World Bank, Agency for International Development (AID), and other U.S. and international agencies.

In 1986, the National Research Council and the National Academy of Sciences published a book on population growth and economic development prepared by a prestigious scholarly group. This "official" report reversed almost completely the frightening conclusions of the previous 1971 National Academy of Sciences (NAS) report. "The scarcity of exhaustible resources is at most a minor constraint on economic growth," it now said. It found benefits of additional people as well as costs. Yes, I know that the conclusions of the report left just enough doubt for AID and others to argue that population growth could be negative. But I believe that any fair-minded reader of that report will observe the breathtaking overturning of the conventional wisdom on the subject.

Even the World Bank reported in 1984 that the world's natural resource situation provided no reason to limit population growth.

Statistical Studies

All the aggregate statistical studies, starting with Kuznets and Easterlin way back in 1967, show that faster population growth does not cause slower economic growth. And all the relevant studies of the underlying relationships—such as saving, education, agricultural investment, and the like—confirm the aggregate studies. One body of research that is particularly interesting in light of the Malthusian history of the subject, shows that all raw materials have become less scarce, not more scarce, defying simplistic Malthusian reasoning.

By 1990, anyone who asserts that population growth damages the economy must either turn a blind eye to the scientific evidence, or be blatantly dishonest intellectually. Hence I am now willing for the first time— and perhaps frustration finally induces me to do so—to use strong language to characterize the doomsayers: they act against human life; they are the enemies of humanity. (In turn, they call people like me enemies of trees and animals. But I make no recommendations that the number of trees or animals should be reduced beyond what individuals choose to do themselves with their own property.)

A Victory Over Death

Let's review a few facts. In the 19th Century the earth could sustain only one billion people. Ten thousand years ago, only 1 million could keep themselves alive. Now, 5 billion people are living longer and more healthily than ever before, on average.

The increase in the world's population represents our victory over death. Two hundred years ago life expectancy in the richest country of the world was less than 30 years at birth; now it is 75. In the poor countries during the past four decades, life expectancy has jumped perhaps 20 years, an incredible gain.

You would expect lovers of humanity to jump with joy at this triumph of human mind and organization over the raw forces of nature. Instead, they lament that there are so many people alive to enjoy the gift of life. And they implement inhumane programs of coercion and denial of personal liberty in one of the most precious choices a family can make—the number of children that it wishes to bear and raise. . .

Forecasts

Every forecast of the doomsayers has been wrong. Metals, foods, and other natural resources have become more available rather than more scarce throughout the centuries. The U.S. famine deaths they forecast we would see on television never occurred. The Great Lakes are not dead; instead they offer better sport fishing than ever. We have not had to worry about "What will we do when the pumps run dry?" The main pollutants, especially the particulates which have killed people for years, have lessened in our cities. But nothing has reduced the doomsayers' credibility with the press or their command over the funding resources of the federal government.

I invite you to test for yourself this assertion that the conditions of humanity have gotten worse. Pick up the *Bureau of the Census's Statistical Abstract of the United States* and *Historical Statistics of the United States* at the nearest library and consult the data. (See index for such topics as pollution, life expectancy, and price indexes plus the individual natural resources) or the measures of human welfare that depend upon physical resources, for the U.S. or for the world as a whole: Food production per person. Availability of natural resources as measured by their prices. The cleanliness of the air we breathe and the water we drink in the U.S. The amount of space per person in our homes, and the presence of such amenities as inside toilets and telephones. Most important, the length of life and the incidence of death. You will find that every single measure shows improvement rather than the deterioration that the doomsayers claim has occurred.

In contrast to the doomsayers, the predictions of "our side" have been correct across the board. I could confidently repeat today the talk I gave on Earth Day in 1970. The only modification I'd make is that I would now be less accepting of family planning programs in India and China.

My comments today do not represent one single voice. My remarks about agriculture and resources represent the consensus of economists in those fields. And the consensus of population economists is now not far from what I have said to you.

Lack of Freedom

The world's problem is not too many people, but lack of political and economic freedom. Powerful evidence comes from pairs of countries that have the same culture and history, and had much the same standard of living when they split apart after World War II—East and West Germany, North and South Korea, Taiwan and China. In each case the centrally planned communist country began with less population "pressure", as measured by density per square kilometer, than did the market-directed economy. And the communist and non-communist countries also started with much the same birth rates. But the market-directed economies have performed much better economically than the centrally planned economies. This powerful explanation of economic development cuts the ground from under population growth as a likely explanation. . .

Global Environment

Blaming population for the problems of countries such as China and Ethiopia is a nasty trick which those who want more government socialism play to advance their own agendas.

Would the environment have gotten cleaner without the exaggerated and untrue scary statements made by the doomsayers starting in the late 1960s? Perhaps they helped speed the cleanup of our air and water—perhaps. Without false alarms, Great Britain started on its cleanup earlier than did the U.S., and went further, faster. But even granting some credit to the doomsayers, were the benefits worth the costs? There were billions wasted in expenditures preparing the airplane industry for $3 per gallon gasoline, and tens of billions wasted worldwide in raw materials purchases made in fear that metal prices would soar out of sight. Much more expensive was the loss of morale and the spirit of adventurous enterprise. Most costly, in my view, has been the inevitable loss of trust in science and in our basic institutions as people realized that they had been systematically fooled. And horribly tragic are the human lives not lived because individuals and countries such as China prevented births in the name of the now-discredited doctrine that population growth slows economic development. The historian will have to balance the questionable benefits against those undeniable costs.

Conclusion

Many people wonder: How can the doomsayers find so many worries when conditions are so much better than in the past? Perhaps the most compelling answer is that there always are potholes in every road. And the potholes should be fixed. The doomsayers can always find potholes, which is a service. But they err in the wrong conclusions they draw from the potholes about the future roads, and what needs to be done.

The doomsayers avoid confronting historical experience by saying that they focus on the future rather than the past. But this is utterly unscientific. Valid science is based on experience; all theories derive from experience and must be tested against it.

12   THE EARTH IN CRISIS

VANISHING FARMLAND: THE POINT

Lester R. Brown

Lester R. Brown is president of the Worldwatch Institute, an environmental research organization based in Washington, D.C.

Points to Consider:

1. How do China's problems illustrate the decline of global grain production?

2. Worldwide, how many tons of topsoil are farmers losing each year?

3. Why does this loss happen?

4. What is the relationship between the global water tables and irrigation?

5. How will technology affect the future world food supply?

6. What policies will best protect future world food supply?

Lester R. Brown, "Drought Deepens Worsening World Food Situation", *Star Tribune*, July 6, 1988.

Worldwide, farmers are losing an estimated 24 billion tons of topsoil each year, roughly the amount of topsoil covering all of Australia's wheat lands.

Grain Production

After two decades of impressive gains, global food production has slowed. The growth of grain production has slowed in several populous countries, including China, India, Indonesia and Mexico. India more than tripled its wheat harvest between 1965 – when the Green Revolution was launched – and 1983; since then, its grain production has not increased at all. In China, the economic reforms that boosted grain production by nearly half between 1976 and 1984 have run out of steam. Beijing recently announced that it was abandoning its goal of regaining the 1984 output level.

China's problems are illustrative. Soil erosion is thinning the topsoil layer, extensive building of new homes is shrinking cropland area, particularly for grain, and fresh water is growing scarce as farmers compete with industry for dwindling supplies.

The loss of momentum in world food output is widespread. The remarkable increases in food production in industrial and developing countries alike over the past 15 years have come in part at the expense of soil and water resources. By definition, farmers can overplow and overpump only in the short run; for many, the short run is now drawing to a close.

The Soil

Deteriorating soils. Since 1950 the world demand for food has nearly tripled. As the demand for food climbed, soil erosion increased, accelerating sharply during the 1970s when world grain prices doubled after the massive Soviet wheat purchase in 1972. Almost overnight, the world's grain stocks were depleted.

In the United States, farmers not only returned idled cropland to use, but they plowed millions of highly erodible acres that should never have been plowed. Between 1972 and 1976, the U.S. grain area expanded some 24 percent. Soil erosion increased far more. By 1976, U.S. farmers were losing an estimated six tons of soil for every ton of grain they produced. The Soviet Union, embarrassed by its agricultural failure, expanded its area in grain by some 7 percent, pushing it to an all-time high in 1977. Throughout the Third World, mounting population pressures were pushing farmers onto lands too steeply sloping to sustain cultivation and semi-arid lands too dry to protect them from the winds.

Perhaps the grimmest soil erosion report came in 1978 when a dispatch from the U.S. Embassy in Addis Abbaba indicated that an estimated 1 billion tons of topsoil were washing down from Ethiopia's highlands each year. Any agronomist could see that Ethiopia was headed for trouble.

By the early 1980s, the inherent productivity of roughly a third of the world's cropland was slowly falling, though increased use of chemical fertilizers often masked this deterioration. Worldwide, farmers are losing an estimated 24 billion tons of topsoil each year, roughly the amount of topsoil covering all of Australia's wheat lands.

Water

Falling water tables. The same price signals and political pressures also led to increased investment in irrigation. Between 1950 and 1982, world irrigated area nearly tripled, going from 232 million acres to 645 million. Some of this expansion was achieved by overpumping. In 1986, the U.S. Department of Agriculture reported that 14 million of the 52 million acres of U.S. irrigated cropland were being watered by pulling down water tables, with the drop ranging from six inches to four feet per year.

China, India and the Soviet Union were also expanding their irrigated areas. In some areas, the additional irrigation appears to be sustainable; but in others, it is not. In India, several states are suffering from falling water tables and wells that are going dry. Thousands of villages now rely on tank trucks for their drinking water. In the Soviet Union, irrigation diversions have sharply reduced the flow into the Aral Sea; as a result the sea is barely half its original size.

There are still opportunities for expanding the world's irrigated area, using both river and underground water, but most of the easy irrigation gains have been made. Increasingly, municipalities and industrial firms will outbid farmers for available water supplies.

Declining Acres

Agricultural retrenchment. Even ignoring cropland idled under U.S. commodity programs, the world area in grain has declined steadily since reaching a record high in 1981. The United States is in the midst of a five-year program to convert at least 40 million acres of highly erodible cropland (11 percent of total cropland) to grassland or woodland before it loses its topsoil and becomes wasteland.

In contrast to the United States, the Soviet Union does not have a program for converting highly erodible land to less-intensive, albeit sustainable, uses. As a consequence, each year since 1977, it has simply abandoned roughly a million hectares (about 2.5 million acres) of cropland, leading to a 13 percent shrinkage in grain area.

In the Third World, cropland degradation from erosion is

71

leading to the wholesale abandonment not only of cropland, but entire villages. In parts of northern Ethiopia, for example, there is simply not enough topsoil to sustain even subsistence-level farming. The result has been recurrent famine.

Across the southern fringe of the Sahara Desert, thousands of villages are being surrendered to the sand. As a result of declining rainfall, land degradation and dune formation, the agricultural frontier is retreating southward across a broad band of Africa, stretching from Mauritania in the west to Sudan in the east.

In recent years, the world's two leading food producers have experienced a decline in irrigation. China's irrigated area has shrunk by some 2 percent since 1978. The U.S. use of irrigation water dropped 9 percent between 1980 and 1985, reversing a longstanding trend. Two years ago, the Soviet government shelved a plan to divert rivers now flowing into the Arctic Ocean southward into central Asia. Although investment in irrigation continues, the prospective net gains are modest ones.

Even as the world's farmers retrench, they face a new challenge with the prospect of global climate change driven by rising concentrations of atmospheric "greenhouse gases". It is not possible to link conclusively this year's drought with the projected long-term warming, but the lower rainfall, higher temperatures and greater evaporation now being experienced in the North American agricultural heartland are consistent with the changes projected by global meteorological models.

Technology

A dwindling backlog of technology. There are no technologies waiting in the wings that will lead to the quantum jumps in world food output of the sort associated with the hybridization of corn, the eightfold increase in fertilizer use between 1950 and 1980, the near tripling of irrigated area during the same period, or the rapid spread of the Green Revolution. The world's farmers are struggling to feed a record 86 million additional people each year, but without any major new technologies to draw upon.

Food Supplies

As world food supplies tighten, the 50 million acres of U.S. cropland idled under commodity programs in 1988 can quickly be returned to production, as was done in 1973. But once this land is back in use, rapid gains in world food output will not come easily.

In the end, future gains in world food supply will depend on arresting and reversing the land degradation that is undermining agriculture in many countries. Restoring the land's fertility is not impossible, but it is difficult and time-consuming. Without a massive reordering of priorities, food scarcity and higher food prices may well dominate the 1990s.

THE EARTH IN CRISIS

VANISHING FARMLAND: THE COUNTERPOINT

Warren T. Brookes

Warren T. Brookes is a syndicated columnist. The following article appeared in the Conservative Chronicle.

Points to Consider:

1. Why does America have the most bountiful food supply in history?

2. Who was Paul Ehrlich and what did he advocate?

3. Why was Lester Brown wrong about his ideas on population and food production?

4. How much farmland has been added to global food production efforts each year?

5. Why has world food production outstripped population gains?

6. What is "low-input agriculture", and why is it a danger to the world's food supply?

Warren T. Brookes, "Farm Chemical Phobia is Dangerous", *Conservative Chronical*, 1990. By permission of Warren T. Brookes and *Creators Syndicate.*

In 1979, Lester Brown was warning of "vanishing farmland". But, as it turned out, the world and the United States were then adding farmland at 3 percent to 5 percent a year.

Americans have every right to be grateful to Mother Nature for the most bountiful food supply in human history.

But some of the gratitude should be reserved for the most advanced agricultural technology in the world, which over the last 50 years has revolutionized the productivity of our food chain.

Sadly, the Luddite leaders of Earth Day seem determined to destroy that technology by forcing the banning of all agricultural chemicals and pesticides or at least drastically limiting their usage through something called "Low Input Sustainable Agriculture" (LISA), recently endorsed by the National Research Council.

Food and Population

Fifty years ago, when we practiced that kind of farming, we paid 26 cents of every dollar for our food, and it took nearly 20 percent of our population to feed us. Today, it takes only 2 percent, as U.S. agri-technology has confounded the hunger mongers worldwide.

In his 1968 book, *The Population Bomb*, Stanford biologist and Earth Day co-founder Paul Ehrlich, said, "The battle to feed humanity is over. In the 1970s, the world will undergo famines, a minimum of 10 million people, most of them children, will starve to death during each year of the 1970s."

Yet, as Dr. Donald Plucknett of the Secretariat of the International Agricultural Research Center told a Hudson Institute conference ("American Agriculture in the '90s") in Indianapolis: "The world has not had a major famine since the end of World War II. Despite rising world population, per capita food production has continued to improve."

Worldwatch

Throughout the 1970s, Worldwatch and Earth Day guru Lester Brown warned of "precipitous declines in the world's food stocks" and growing capacity. In 1974, Brown said that improved seed varieties—the "green revolution"—would not increase world food production, which he said would fall behind population growth. Instead, as then State Department (now Hudson Institute) agri-economist Dennis Avery told Congress last September, "Since 1974, the world's average yield of wheat has increased 36 percent—World rice yields have increased 38 percent—Coarse grain yields have risen 30 percent. These

┌───┐
│ **WARMING COULD HELP FARMERS** │
│ │
│ *Farmers could benefit from global warming, according to* │
│ *the most elaborate analysis ever made of the impact of the* │
│ *greenhouse effect on U.S. agriculture.* │
│ │
│ Washington Post, *May 18, 1990* │
└───┘

yields were enough to produce global surpluses.

No wonder Brown wouldn't testify with Avery and refused to participate in the Hudson conference. But, he warned that growing food yields are based on "unsustainable reliance on chemicals and the farming of marginal erodible lands." Yet, Plucknett says, "Since 1960, the gains in food production have been achieved without significant expansion of crops into forest land or fragile soils."

Furthermore, the United States is one of the lowest and most efficient users of agricultural chemicals per acre of any major Western country. West Germany, for example, uses nearly seven times as much fertilizer per acre and three times as much pesticide. But that intensity shows, as German wheat yields are nearly three times as high as ours. Our vast acreage allows a less intensive agriculture than Europe's.

Vanishing Farmland?

Yet, in 1979, Lester Brown was warning of "vanishing farmland". But, as it turned out, the world and the United States were then adding farmland at 3 percent to 5 percent a year. By 1985, we had to pay farmers to take 30 percent out of production just to stop the world's food gluts, as the United States led the "green revolution" in biotechnology.

Plucknett points out, "The key to all these gains has been the success of agricultural science. The payoff from agricultural research has been extremely high, both in terms of forestalling hunger and in bringing down the real cost of food in most countries."

Dr. Avery told Congress, "We are living in the golden age of the plant breeder who has produced a wide variety of new seeds that can make better use of soil, sunlight and plant nutrients than any seeds in the previous history of mankind. As a result, world food production has been outstripping population gains even as we pass through the historic peaks of population expansion."

Organic Farming

The environmental lobby is openly anti-population growth. This may explain why the green revolution of biotechnology is now under such vicious attack from the "greens," who are pushing the Environmental Protection Agency to ban more chemicals.

Dr. Alvin Young, head of the U.S. Department of Agriculture's office of biotechnology, says the costs of this assault could be bigger than we think:; "We are now regulating pesticides on the presumption that we have this huge food surplus and we can afford to cut back production. But that surplus doesn't exist anymore. If we wipe out pesticide use, we will slash U.S. food output by at least 40 percent."

Said Young: "Organic farming is fine for one- or two- or even 10-acre plots, but for commercial, low-labor farming, we couldn't provide the food for this country's needs. The phobia about food chemicals could easily be disastrous to our entire food production industry."

As Nobel prize-winning agronomist Norman Borlaug pointed out in 1988, the low-input agriculture practices of the 1930s were barely adequate to feed a world of 2 billion people, let alone the 5 billion we now have: "To return to the methods of 50 years ago would plunge the world into famine and into social, economic, political and, yes, environmental chaos."

EXAMINING COUNTERPOINTS

This activity may be used as an individual study guide for students in libraries and resource centers or as a discussion catalyst in small group and classroom discussions.

The Point

The Florida citrus industry is again recovering from a devastating freeze. The 1980s were the worst decade for such freezes this century, climaxing a long decline in Southern winter temperatures.

In 1900, the northern panhandle of Florida was the center of citrus growing, and Georgia and Louisiana were still major citrus producers. But successive cooling has driven growers 200 to 300 miles south, and even so, survival is getting tougher.

Similar trends of agriculture being driven south, not north, can be found from Georgia to Texas. A growing body of students of weather data say when you look at rural readings, alone, without the polluting effect of urbanization, there has been no warming.

In fact, the only U.S. temperature record that does that, the National Reference Climatological Network, not only shows a long-term cooling in the United States, but it shows the decade of the 1980s as unusually cold, not hot. (Warren T. Brookes, *Human Events*, February 17, 1990.)

The Counterpoint

The six hottest years on record have all occurred in the last decade.

That fact, plus recent droughts and heat waves, has called attention to a major threat to our environment: an unprecedented trend of global temperature increases caused by the "greenhouse effect".

This global warming is believed to be the result of the growing release of heat-trapping gases into the atmosphere. Climatologists predict that global temperatures could rise by as much as nine degrees (F) by the year 2050 — an increase far greater and more rapid then any in history.

Even a smaller rise could have terrible consequences:

agricultural disasters, extinction of animal and plant species, and severe damage to coastlines from rising seas. . .

But civilization is now adding to the concentrations of greenhouse gases in the atmosphere, apparently causing the earth's temperature to rise beyond its natural level. (Union of Concerned Scientists, January 1990.)

Guidelines

Social issues are usually complex, but often problems become oversimplified in political debates and discussion. Usually a polarized version of social conflict does not adequately represent the diversity of views that surround social conflicts.

1. Examine the counterpoints above. Then write down other possible interpretations of this issue than the two arguments stated in the counterpoints above.

2. How do you interpret the cartoon on page 28. Does its editorial message support either the point or the counter-point?

CHAPTER 3

ECOLOGY AND HUMAN VALUES

14. GROWTH IS KILLING THE ENVIRONMENT   82

    Murray Bookchin

15. ECONOMIC GROWTH IS THE SOLUTION   89

    Gro Harlem Brundtland

16. THE ENVIRONMENTAL ELITE'S   93
    ATTACK ON FREE ENTERPRISE

    Capital Research Center

17. ACCOUNTING FOR A HEALTHY   99
    ENVIRONMENT

    James Robertson

18. DEEP ECOLOGY AND ECOTERRORISM   105
    THREATEN OUR FUTURE

    Doug Bandow

19. DEEP ECOLOGY: PRESERVING THE   111
    NATURAL ORDER

    Fritjof Capra

14 ECOLOGY AND HUMAN VALUES

GROWTH IS KILLING THE ENVIRONMENT

Murray Bookchin

Murray Bookchin lives in Burlington, Vermont, and is director emeritus of the Institute for Social Ecology at Plainfield, Vermont. He is a contributor to many publications and the author of more than a dozen books, including The Ecology of Freedom *and more recently,* Remaking Society, *published by South End Press.*

Points to Consider:

1. Why is the word "accident" inappropriate for describing ecological disasters like the *Exxon-Valdez* oil spill?

2. What is meant by saying that the global ecological crisis is "systemic"?

3. How is economic growth related to the market?

4. Describe the reasons and causes for economic growth.

5. What is "social ecology" and how can it help solve environmental problems?

Reprinted by permission from *The Progressive,* 409 East Main Street, Madison, Wisconsin 53703.

Perhaps the most obvious of our systemic problems is uncontrollable growth.

We tend to think of environmental catastrophes—such as the recent *Exxon-Valdez* oil spill disaster in the Bay of Alaska—as "accidents": Isolated phenomena that erupt without notice or warning. But when does the word *accident* become inappropriate? When are such occurrences inevitable rather than accidental? And when does a consistent pattern of inevitable disasters point to a deep-seated crisis that is not only environmental but profoundly social? . .

A Systemic Problem

What environmentalists must emphasize is that the global ecological crisis is *systemic*, not simply the product of random mishaps. If the *Exxon-Valdez* disaster is treated merely as an "accident"—as were Chernobyl and Three Mile Island—we will have deflected public attention from a social crisis of historic proportions: we do not simply live in a world of problems but in a highly problematical world, an *inherently* anti-ecological society. This anti-ecological world will not be healed by acts of statesmanship or passage of piecemeal legislation. It is a world that it is direly in need of far-reaching structural change.

Perhaps the most obvious of our systemic problems is uncontrollable growth. I use the word "uncontrollable" advisedly, in preference to "uncontrolled." The growth of which I speak is not humanity's colonization of the planet over millennia of history. It is rather an inexorable material reality that is unique to our era: namely, that *unlimited* economic growth is assumed to be evidence of human progress. We have taken this notion so much for granted over the past few generations that it is as immutably fixed in our consciousness as the sanctity of property itself.

Growth is, in fact, almost synonymous with the market economy that prevails today. That fact finds its clearest expression in the marketplace maxim, "Grow or die." We live in a competitive world in which rivalry is a law of economic life. . .

Beyond Control

It's not enough, however, to blame our environmental problems on the obsession with growth. A system of deeply entrenched structures— of which growth is merely a surface manifestation—makes up our society. These structures are beyond moral control, much as the flow of adrenaline is beyond the control of a frightened creature. This system has, in effect, the commanding quality of natural law.

In a national or international market society (be it of the corporate kind found in the West or the bureaucratic kind found

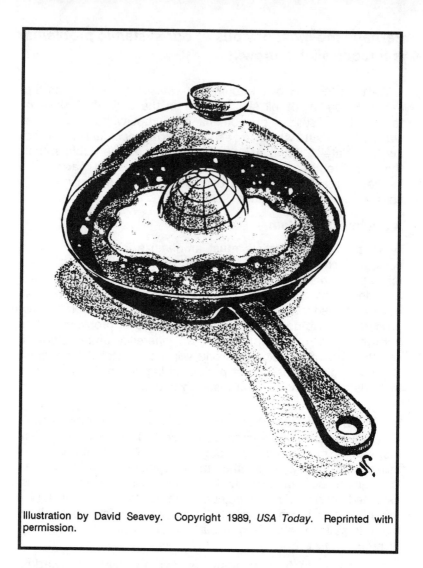

Illustration by David Seavey. Copyright 1989, *USA Today*. Reprinted with permission.

in the East), competition itself generates a need for growth. Growth is each enterprise's defense against the threat of absorption by a rival. Moral issues have no bearing on this compelling adversarial relationship. To the extent that a market economy becomes so pervasive that it turns society itself into a marketplace—a vast shopping mall—it dictates the moral parameters of human life and makes growth synonymous with personal as well as social progress. One's personality, love life, income, or body of beliefs, no less than an enterprise, must grow or die.

This market society seems to have obliterated from most people's memory another world that once placed limits on growth, stressed cooperation over competition, and valued that gift as a bond of human solidarity. In that remote world, that market was marginal to a domestic or "natural" society. . .

It has been dawning on the First World, which is rapidly using up many of its resources, that growth is eating away the biosphere at a pace unprecedented in human history. Deforestation from acid rain, itself a product of fossil fuel combustion, is matched or even exceeded by the systematic burning that is clearing vast rain forests. The destruction of the ozone layer, we are beginning to learn, is occurring almost everywhere, not just in Antarctica.

We now sense that unlimited growth is literally recycling the complex organic products of natural evolution into the simple mineral constituents of the earth at the dawn of life billions of years ago. Soil that was in the making for millennia is being turned into sand; richly forested regions filled with complex life forms are being reduced to barren moonscapes; rivers, lakes, and even vast oceanic regions are becoming noxious and lethal sewers; radio-nuclides, together with an endless and ever-increasing array of toxicants, are invading the air we breathe, the water we drink, and almost every food item on the dinner table. Not even sealed, air-conditioned, and sanitized offices are immune to that poisonous deluge.

Economic Growth

Growth is only the most immediate cause of this pushing back of the evolutionary clock to a more primordial and mineralized world. And calling for "limits to growth" is merely the first step toward bringing the magnitude of our environmental problems under public purview. Unless growth is traced to its basic source — competition in a grow-or-die market society — the demand for controlling growth is meaningless as well as unattainable. We can no more arrest growth while leaving the market intact than we can arrest egoism while leaving rivalry intact.

In this hidden world of cause-and-effect, the environmental movement and the public stand at a crossroads. Is growth a product of "consumerism" — the most socially acceptable and socially neutral explanation that we usually encounter in discussions of environmental deterioration? Or does growth occur because of the nature of production for a market economy? To a certain extent, we can say, both. But the overall reality of a market economy is that consumer demand for a new product rarely occurs spontaneously, nor is its consumption guided purely by personal considerations.

Today, demand is created not by consumers but by producers — specifically, by enterprises called advertising agencies that use a host of techniques to manipulate public taste. American washing and drying machines, for example, are all but constructed to be used communally — and they are communally used in many apartment buildings. Their privatization in homes, where they stand idle most of the time, is a result of advertising ingenuity.

Population Increase

One can survey the entire landscape of typical "consumer" items and find many other examples of the irrational consumption of products by individuals and small families — "consumer" items that readily lend themselves to public use.

Another popular explanation of the environmental crisis is population increase. This argument would be more compelling if it could be shown that countries with the largest rates of population increase are the largest consumers of energy, raw material, or even food. But such correlations are notoriously false. . .

We have yet to determine how many people the planet can sustain without complete ecological disruption. The data are far from conclusive, but they are surely highly biased — generally along economic, racial, and social lines. Demography is far from a science, but it is a notorious political weapon whose abuse has disastrously claimed the lives of millions over the course of the century.

Technology

Finally, "industrial society", to use a genteel euphemism for capitalism, has also become an easy explanation for the environmental ills that afflict our time. But a blissful ignorance clouds the fact that several centuries ago, much of England's forest land, including Robin Hood's legendary haunts, was deforested by the crude axes of rural proletarians to produce charcoal for a technologically simple metallurgical economy and to clear land for profitable sheep runs. This occurred long before the Industrial Revolution.

Technology may magnify a problem or even accelerate its effects. But with or without a "technological imagination" (to use Jacques Ellul's expression), rarely does it produce the problem itself. Indeed, the rationalization of work by means of assembly-line techniques goes back to such patently pre-industrial societies as the pyramid-builders of ancient Egypt, who developed a vast human machine to build temples and mausoleums.

Privatizing Problems

To take growth out of its proper social context is to distort and privatize the problem. It is inaccurate and unfair to coerce people into believing that they are *personally* responsible for present-day ecological dangers because they consume too much or proliferate too readily.

This privatization of the environmental crisis, like New Age cults that focus on personal problems rather than on social dislocations, has reduced many environmental movements to utter ineffectiveness and threatens to diminish their credibility with the public. If "simple living" and militant recycling are the main solutions to the environmental crisis, the crisis will certainly continue and intensify.

Ironically, many ordinary people and their families cannot afford to live "simply". It is a demanding enterprise when one considers the costliness of "simple" hand-crafted artifacts and the exorbitant price of organic and "recycled" goods. Moreover, what the "production end" of the environmental crisis cannot sell to the "consumption end", it will certainly sell to the military. General Electric enjoys considerable eminence not only for its refrigerators but also for the Gatling guns. This shadowy side of the environmental problem — military production — can only be ignored by attaining an ecological airheadedness so vacuous as to defy description.

Causes of Growth

Public concern for the environment cannot be addressed by placing the blame on growth without spelling out the causes of growth. Nor can an explanation be exhausted by citing "consumerism" while ignoring the sinister role played by rival producers in shaping public taste and guiding public purchasing power. Aside from the costs involved, most people quite rightly do not want to "live simply". They do not want to diminish their freedom to travel or their access to culture, or to scale down needs that often serve to enrich human personality and sensitivity.

It will take a high degree of sensitivity and

reflection—attributes that are fostered by the consumption of such items as books, art works, and music—to gain an understanding of what one ultimately needs and does not need to be a truly fulfilled person. Without such people in sufficient numbers to challenge the destruction of the planet, the environmental movement will be as superficial in the future as it is ineffectual today. . .

By what criteria are we to determine what constitutes needless growth, for example, and what is needful growth? Who will make this decision—state agencies, town meetings, alliances among towns on a county-wide basis, neighborhoods in cities?

Social Ecology

New Age environmentalism and conventional environmentalism that place limits on serious, in-depth ecological thinking have been increasingly replaced by social ecology that explores the economic and institutional factors that enter into the environmental crisis.

In the context of this more mature discourse, the Valdez oil spill is no longer seen as an Alaskan matter, an "episode" in the geography of pollution. Rather it is recognized as a social act that raises such "accidents" to the level of systemic problems—rooted not in consumerism, technological advance, and population growth but in an irrational system of production, an abuse of technology by a grow-or-die economy, and the demographics of poverty and wealth. Ecological dislocation cannot be separated from social dislocations.

The social roots of our environmental problems cannot remain hidden without trivializing the crisis itself and thwarting its resolution.

15   ECOLOGY AND HUMAN VALUES

ECONOMIC GROWTH IS THE SOLUTION

Gro Harlem Brundtland

Gro Harlem Brundtland was Norway's Prime Minister from 1986 to 1989 and Minister of Environment from 1974 to 1979. She is currently the leader of Norway's Labor Party.

Points to Consider:

1. Why is poverty the biggest polluter?

2. How is sustainable development defined?

3. Why is economic growth needed?

4. How must poor nations be helped by rich nations?

5. How can the environment be protected while economic growth takes place?

Gro Harlen Bruntland, "Growth Is Good", *Mother Jones* April/May 1990.

Only growth can create the capacity we need to overcome the environmental crisis.

Time has proved the truth of Indira Gandhi's words: "Poverty is the biggest polluter." In the Third World we have seen time and time again that the poor have no alternative in their daily struggle for survival than to overuse the environmental and natural resources. Even in the industrialized nations, poverty and lack of resources are often used – and misused – as an argument for not starting necessary cleanup operations to correct mistakes against our natural environment.

Sustainable Development

The World Commission on Environment and Development (a United Nations-sponsored body chaired by Brundtland in 1987) offered the concept of sustainable development as the best strategy to obtain this global reorientation. Sustainable development is a broad concept of social and economic progress. It permits us to meet the needs and aspirations of the present generation without compromising the ability of future generations to meet their needs.

In the 1990s we will need a global consensus for economic growth. In its report, *Our Common Future*, the World Commission stated very clearly that:

- Growth, but growth that is equally distributed, is essential if we are to pull the destitute millions out of the poverty trap.
- Only growth can create the capacity we need to overcome the environmental crisis.

Sustainable global development requires that those who are more affluent adopt life-styles that are within the planet's ecological means. There is tremendous potential in energy efficiency. We need to agree on regional strategies for stabilizing and reducing emissions that threaten the atmosphere. We must strongly intensify our efforts to develop renewable forms of energy.

A New Era

A new era of sustainable growth cannot take place without an intimate linking of environmental and economic activities. We need political reform and real options for making informed choices. The corollary must be that those responsible for activities that have an impact on a nation's environment and resource base must assume responsibility and accountability for the environment as well as for the economic dimensions.

A special effort must be made to assist the developing countries. They clearly need our help in avoiding the same mistakes that we have made toward our natural environment.

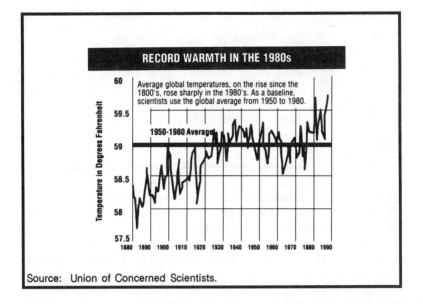

RECORD WARMTH IN THE 1980s

Average global temperatures, on the rise since the 1800's, rose sharply in the 1980's. As a baseline, scientists use the global average from 1950 to 1980.

1950-1980 Average

Temperature in Degrees Fahrenheit

Source: Union of Concerned Scientists.

We are under a clear duty to redouble our efforts to help the Third World lay off the chains of poverty, devastating debts, and ever-worsening environmental degradation. On a global basis, we need to have open markets, improved commodity prices, and stable exchange rates. The developing countries will need a transfer of technology on better terms than today's, particularly in the field of energy-efficient technology.

At a time when the need for assistance is growing, it is both politically and morally unacceptable that there is still a net transfer of resources from the poor countries to the rich. The industrialized nations should make a firm commitment to secure genuine additional financial resources as a compensation to poor counties in their struggle for adjustment to sustainable development patterns.

At the start of the 1990s, all of us who served on the World Commission are heartened by the extent to which the ideas brought forward in its report, *Our Common Future*, have been accepted throughout the world in the past three years. Governments, international institutions, nongovernmental organizations, and elements of the media all over the world have proclaimed fervent attachment to the principle of sustainable development. We are in the middle of an active follow-up program that will take us to the 1992 UN Conference on Environment and Development in Brazil. By then, we must be ready as a world community to take radical, far-reaching, and unified action.

Global Climate

The climate issue is vital. Life on earth depends on it. A

global climate agreement should be negotiated in time for a signing at the 1992 conference. To succeed we must establish effective instruments for a strong monitoring medium and be willing to accept broad majority decisions on sustainable standards and regulations. Effective steps to curb the threats to the world climate are going to cost money. We should establish a climate fund as proposed by the Norwegian government last year, with industrialized countries' contributions on the order of 0.1 percent of gross national product, or through levying a user's tax on emissions or on the use of fossil fuels.

We know the signs of the global crisis now under way. The mass extinction of species, the relentless destruction of forests, massive desertification, soil erosion, acidification, ozone depletion, global warming, the ever-greater burdens we place on the world's poorest and weakest — all cry out for a global reorientation of the way we manage human affairs.

In an age when more and more decisions are lifted outside of national control through the process of internationalization, we need to give more authority to our international institutions to arrive at a better management of interdependence. We need a stronger, revitalized United Nations to promote a truly global perspective for our efforts toward the year 2000 and beyond.

16 ECOLOGY AND HUMAN VALUES

THE ENVIRONMENTAL ELITE'S ATTACK ON FREE ENTERPRISE

Capital Research Center

The Capital Research Center in Washington, D.C., describes itself as a non-partisan educational and research organization.

Points to Consider:

1. Who are the "environmental elite" and what have they done?

2. How do they endanger jobs and economic growth?

3. Why are environmentalists an elite group?

4. Identify the corporations that have given money to environmental groups.

"The Environmental Elite's Attack on Free Enterprise", *Organization Trends*, April, 1990. A publication of the Capital Research Center in Washington, D.C.

Environmental activists endanger the almost universal public interest in jobs and economic growth.

The first Earth Day produced the Environmental Protection Agency and helped shape the modern environmental movement into a powerful force for ever-increasing legislative and regulatory control of business and the environment at the expense of the individual American taxpayer.

Like the environment itself, many of the environmental activist movement's leading organizations have evolved into something significantly different from what their founders envisioned. The Sierra Club, set up by mountaineers in 1982 to "explore, enjoy, and render accessible the mountain regions of the Pacific Coast," has deleted any mention of "accessibility" in its bylaws, and in 1988 the directors placed a ban on any Club-sponsored mountain climbing expeditions which require ropes or ice axes, effectively terminating its original purpose. This leaves more time and energy for the intense political activism so characteristic of today's organization. . .

Public or Special Interest?

Beyond the questions raised by these changes in direction and purpose, the environmental elite's claim to represent something called the "public interest" is extremely dubious. First, finding the "public interest" in a nation of 250 million people with a wide range of desires and opinions is not as easy as those who use the phrase would like us to believe. Even if we accept the validity of the concept, environmental activists endanger the almost universal public interest in jobs and economic growth.

In the Pacific Northwest, where many jobs depend on the timber industry, environmental special interests have worked to prevent the cutting of old growth forests. Finding no law—that is to say, no democratically voiced sentiment—against cutting down old-growth trees, the movement created the issue of the spotted owl, pressuring the U.S. Fish and Wildlife Service to add this unendangered bird to its list of endangered species and thereby prohibit actions harmful to its environment, such as cutting the timber in the area. As Andy Stahl of the Sierra Club explained, "The northern spotted owl is the wildlife species of choice to act as a surrogate for old-growth protection."

In the resource Conservation and Recovery Act, which governs the storage of hazardous wastes, the Clean Air Act, and the Clean Water Act, environmentalists push for standards well beyond the necessities for human safety, and at great economic cost. Abroad, the American environmental movement seeks to impose international restrictions that many Third World countries fear could impede their development. Brazil is especially

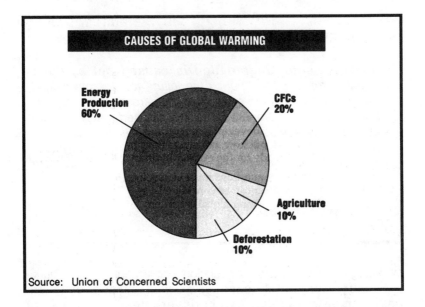

CAUSES OF GLOBAL WARMING

Energy Production 60%

CFCs 20%

Agriculture 10%

Deforestation 10%

Source: Union of Concerned Scientists

incensed over international efforts to halt development of the Amazon rain forests.

Demographically, the environmental movement clearly does not represent the American populace. Approximately 50 percent of the Sierra Club's membership has an annual income of $50,000 or above (nationally, only 18.5 percent of households, which are often two-income, match this figure) and the average member's home has a value of over $187,000, twice the national average. As one Sierra Club writer admitted: "It's getting tougher all the time to spot the tree-hugger lurking within the well-educated, well-compensated, middle-aged, professional whose image the survey conjures up."

The Unfinished Agenda

Far from being tribunes of the people, members of the environmental movement are a decidedly elite group with a special interest that conflicts in many cases with the economic interests of less affluent groups. The biases of this group—political control of the environment through government legislation and regulation at the expense of private, free-market action—was clearly articulated in 1977 in *The Unfinished Agenda* and is still quite discernible in the *Blueprint for the Environment,* presented to President-elect George Bush in 1988.

The *Unfinished Agenda,* produced by a task force including representatives from the twelve largest environmental activist organizations, is based on the assumption that the industrialized world's material prosperity is "built on abundant supplies of easily accessible energy and minerals [and] now appears to be approaching a period of materials scarcity." The report calls for an anti-growth agenda of "population stabilization", redistribution of wealth "for moral reasons, as well as economic and environmental ones," and government controls on industrialization, such as "strict zoning on either the federal or state level to conserve prime agricultural land for agricultural purposes only."

Significantly, the report argued for the relative unimportance of private property rights when "public rights" were threatened, a philosophy which justifies the report's legacy of public land acquisitions — often through confiscation or "taking" under the eminent domain power — by the Land and Water Conservation Fund, American Heritage Trust, and "buffer" zones around national parks.

To further ensure "public rights", and to make up for the private sector's "relatively short time horizon", the report's authors recommend national planning of the economy, including a National Planning Board with oversight from a Presidential commission including environmentalists, and charging the Environmental Protection Agency with monitoring "the explicit and implicit environmental message contained in both the programming and commercials on television."

Blueprint for Environment, a 1500-page tome of over 500 specific recommendations for the President, updates the environmental activist agenda while retaining the basic pro-government, anti-private sector stance. Like *The Unfinished Agenda,* it is a consensus document, produced by over 100 groups on 32 task forces, the consensus being that government must significantly expand its activities and funding in population control, both at home and abroad, on land acquisition and protection, and on such activities as matching grants "to be used for hiring state coordinators of environmental education programs" and an EPA Aquafund to complement Superfund.

The *Blueprint* seeks a wide range of intrusive federal regulations, including "national water efficiency standards for plumbing fixtures and products" and "standards to reduce the amount of electric energy consumed by fluorescent and incandescent lamps." It seeks a 10-cent/per gallon gasoline tax, with 10 percent of the proceeds "designated for low-income needs", and fuel-efficiency standards to mandate 45-miles-per-gallon cars by the year 2000.

Corporate Support

Signing on to this plea for significant government expansion were representatives from all the major environmental activist organizations, including the Sierra Club, National Wildlife Federation, Natural Resources Defense Council, National Audubon Society, and Izaak Walton League of America. This has by no means prevented corporations from sponsoring these organizations.

Among the Audubon Society's contributors in 1987-1988 were Stroh's and the Turner Broadcasting System, each contributing over $50,000; Waste Management, Inc. and the Times Mirror Foundation, which gave over $25,000; and a number of corporations donating over $10,000, including GTE, General Electric, and Morgan Stanley and Company. Both the Sierra Club and the Natural Resources Defense Council have drawn support from major banks: Chemical Bank and Morgan Bank respectively.

The National Wildlife Federation has drawn support from ARCO, Amoco, Exxon, Mobil, Monsanto, and Waste Management, Inc., all of whom can expect their activities to be even more heavily regulated by government if the *Blueprint's* recommendations are enacted. The Izaak Walton League's executive director, Jack Lorenz, boasts that the League "has the longest history of tough positions regarding industry's impacts on the environment—while also having solid corporate support through contributions."

Earthfest '90

The Annapolis Foundation, a fledgling organization with close ties to the National Association of Manufacturers (NAM), is seeking to raise money for the EPA's Earthfest '90, an exhibit of "environmentally sound" corporate exhibits screened by environmental activist groups. Characteristically, many environmentalists were suspicious of businesses being involved in an Earth Day exhibit. "We had some concerns," said Christina Dawson, executive director of Earth Day 1990, "that the very industries the EPA is charged with regulating would be paying for an event that was sponsored by the EPA." Ms. Dawson, of course, sees no conflict of interest in EPA giving grants to establishment environmental groups which often lobby Congress on EPA activities and funding.

In fact, there is legitimate reason to wonder about the decision, not of the EPA to seek NAM funding, but of the NAM to align itself so closely to Earth Day, which is sure to be a festival of anti-business agitation. Corporations need to understand that the establishment environmental movement of today has concluded that heavy regulation of business by government is the preferable, and possibly the only, way to protect the environment.

When Jay D. Hair, President of the National Wildlife Federation, says of the accidental oil spill in Prince William Sound, "This is a classic example of the disease of corporate greed. Big oil, big lies," it is not only the oil companies that should reconsider their financial ties to the environmental elite.

17 ECOLOGY AND HUMAN VALUES

ACCOUNTING FOR A HEALTHY ENVIRONMENT

James Robertson

James Robertson works as an independent writer, speaker and consultant on economic and social change.

Points to Consider:

1. How are the words "economy" and "ecology" defined?

2. Why does conventional economics have an accounting problem?

3. Describe the economic problems in poor nations.

4. Define the basic nature of a new economic order.

5. What steps must be taken to achieve a new economic order?

James Robertson, "The New Economics", *Greenpeace,* January/February 1989.

In short, conventional economics now conflicts with social as well as ecological needs, with fairness and justice, with religious and spiritual values, and with common sense.

Economy, like ecology, derives its meaning from the Greek work "oikos," which means house or home. Once compatible, these two words are now in conflict. Literally, ecology is the study or science of our home, and economics refers to its management. Our home is, of course, the earth. But our management of this home, our economy, is destroying it. . .

Accounting Problems

Conventional economics has an accounting problem. It makes no distinction between useful production, such as day care and affordable housing, and that sector of the economy that could be considered damaging, such as cigarettes and junk food. It often gives no value to things that are obviously good. Creating conditions that foster true wealth—the protection of human and environmental health and the treatment of sickness, for example—are counted as wealth consumption, not wealth creation.

Consequently, our traditional accounting measure, the gross national product (GNP), often goes up even when things go wrong. The $70 billion spent in the U.S. last year on pollution abatement boosts the GNP, as does medical spending on injuries resulting from hazardous working conditions or unsafe products. The world market price of wood from rain forests, to give another example, does not include the cost of widespread deforestation to the health of the ecosystem and consequently, to the people. "The social costs of a polluted environment, disrupted communities, disrupted family life and eroded primary relationships may be the only part of the GNP that is growing," says economist Hazel Henderson. "We have no idea whether we are going forward or backward."

Moreover, developments that really do serve the wealth of the public are neglected, discounted or even posted as debits on the national "balance sheet". For example, if by learning to help ourselves and one another, we reduce our dependence, and therefore our spending, on commercial products, professional services and public welfare, the GNP will register a fall. Economists will then tell us we are worse off.

Poor Nations

Conventional economics, obsessed as it is with gross national product and global commodity prices, does not account for the problems posed by lack of local control and self-reliance. Cities

Illustration by Carol*Simpson

and Third World nations today find themselves vulnerably dependent on outside sources of food, energy, technology and other necessities. This dependence means that if something goes awry in the global marketplace or in the financial centers of the U.S. or Europe, people in remote corners of the planet suffer. When Brazil, following the advice of economic experts from the developed world, invested heavily in palm oil plantations, it found its well-being tied to the global price fluctuations of palm oil. As production went up, the price went down, and people in certain parts of Brazil found themselves worse off than before.

The choice of what technologies to pursue, when governed purely by the market, is equally myopic. Benign technologies, such as soft energy technologies, organic farming methods, and other socially and ecologically desirable production methods, are given no economic value for the social benefits they provide. In agricultural research and development, for example, the pursuit of profit has provoked private industry to devote inordinate efforts to fashioning pesticide-resistant plants—a development that could lead to dangerous increases in pesticide use around the world.

The debt crisis offers another lesson in the moral and conceptual bankruptcy of our economic structure. The lending binge of the '70s, which transferred hundreds of billions of dollars from the First to the Third World, has had a devastating backlash. Interest payments on these loans are often half or more of a country's entire annual foreign earnings.

The net flow of money has now reversed itself; some $130 billion net (repayment minus new loans) moved from Latin

America back into the coffers of Northern banks between 1982 and 1987 alone. And, at the insistence of the development agencies, debtor nations are tightening their belts in order to avoid defaulting on these loans, leading to an end to food subsidies and essential public services in already poverty-stricken countries. That an economically devastated continent like Africa could become a net supplier of capital to the developed North at the price of starving its people is, at the very least, a moral outrage.

It is clear that economics has divorced itself from moral and ethical considerations. Vast inequalities in wealth are ignored or justified by adherence to "free market" principles, and corporate criminals who steal millions of dollars or contribute to the health problems of entire communities are almost never brought to justice.

In short, conventional economics now conflicts with social as well as ecological needs, with fairness and justice, with religious and spiritual values, and with common sense. For increasing numbers of us, whether we support the environmental movement, the public health movement, the peace movement, the Third World development movement, the alternative technology movement or a religious faith, conventional economics is a problem, an obstacle, a threat, which we simply cannot ignore.

A New Order

In designing a new economic order, we should ensure that it includes certain key features. First of all, it should acknowledge that economics is not value-free; that moral choices can and must be made based on considerations of equality, justice and simple compassion. It should, therefore, value the conservation of resources and the environment while also accounting for the thousands of useful and rewarding activities that do not conform to the "production/consumption model".

A new economics should recognize the right and responsibility of people to act as moral agents in the economic sphere, and it should enlarge their ability to meet their own needs and control their economic lives. It should make its prime concern the wealth and well-being of the people and the earth, rather than the corporation or the nation. . .

Finally, a new accounting system should include the environmental and social costs of development. Instead of relying on the Gross National Product as a guide to economic health, the new economics must consider the effect a particular action has on the local and global environment and on the health and well-being of employees and people. Research and development will thus shift to technologies that contribute to true "wealth", and the true cost of doing business will be added to the price of commodities.

No Utopian Dream

The establishment of a new economic order is not a utopian dream. In fact, two highly respected international bodies have moved to establish some of the tenets of the new economics in their work.

In 1987, the World Commission on Environment and Development Publication published the Brundtland Report, entitled *Our Common Future.* The commission found that "The time has come to break out of past patterns. . . .Economics and ecology must be completely integrated in decision making and lawmaking processes, not just to protect the environment but also to protect and promote development." This integration of ecological and economic goals would be "best secured by decentralizing the management of resources upon which local communities depend, and giving those communities an effective say over the use of these resources."

The authors of the report recognize that we can't expect African villagers to refrain from cutting trees for fuelwood unless they have the right to control the future use of the trees. By the same token, we shouldn't be surprised if Third World countries, dependent on the sale of their resources to service foreign debt, put their environment at risk to secure short-term economic survival. The destruction of rain forests and the international trade in toxic waste, to cite two examples, point up the type of risks developing nations are prepared to take in order to earn foreign capital. . .

At the personal level, we must exercise more power and responsibility over where our money comes from and where it goes. Ethical investing, conscious purchasing and boycotts are proving to be powerful influences on the course of capital. We can set up a virtuous circle here: if we use our money power in support of our values, the economy will bend to allow an easier and more effective use of our money power.

At the institutional level, the attention given to the management of both the international economy and local economies must be raised to the level now devoted to national economies. The International Fund for Agricultural Development has already found that small direct loans to groups at the village level have a payback rate of 85 to 100 percent. Compare this to the problems of lending to Zaire, for example, which pays less than 20 percent of the annual interest on its loans, and whose ruler, Mobutu Sese Soku, stands accused of stealing $5 billion from his country.

Pressure Groups

Through the 1990s, pressure groups and campaigning organizations like Greenpeace will have to take the lead in promoting the shift to a new economic order. We must insist that governments, businesses, banks, universities, scientific and professional bodies and other established institutions wake up to the need for fundamental change.

As co-founder of one such group, The Other Economic Summit and the New Economics Foundation, which is associated with it, I have a vision for the year 2000. It is that the world leaders will call a historic summit meeting to mark the beginning of the new millennium; to confirm their support for the new 21st century economic order, which by then will already be taking shape; and to pledge themselves and their governments to the creation of a new kind of wealth, synonymous with well-being for people and for the earth. It is a vision that can and must come true. We need to start working and living for it now.

18   ECOLOGY AND HUMAN VALUES

DEEP ECOLOGY AND ECOTERRORISM THREATEN OUR FUTURE

Doug Bandow

Doug Bandow prepared this essay for the Heritage Foundation. He is a Senior Fellow at the Cato Institute in Washington, D.C.

Points to Consider:

1. Identify the roots of ecoterrorism.

2. Define the "Earth First!" movement.

3. Explain the kinds of ecoterrorism that radical groups engage in.

4. How can ecoterrorism be dealt with?

Doug Bandow, "Ecoterrorism: The Dangerous Fringe of the Environmental Movement," The Heritage Foundation Backgrounder, April 12, 1990.

If Deep Ecology is not challenged at the philosophical level, the number of environmentalists committed to ecotage is likely to grow.

As the twentieth anniversary of Earth Day approaches, environmental activists and private citizens alike are reflecting on the state of the earth's ecology and what policies best can make the world cleaner. One environmental matter, however, is receiving little attention. Individuals and scattered bands of environmental or ecological radicals, usually called ecoterrorists, have been sabotaging industrial facilities, logging operations, construction projects, and other economic targets around the country. They have inflicted millions of dollars in damage and have maimed innocent people.

These ecoterrorists are a tiny, fringe group. They in no way represent America's broad environmental movement. Yet, mainstream environmentalists and the press remain strangely silent about the atrocities committed by the ecoterrorists. By failing to police their own movement, and by failing to denounce loudly and openly the ecoterrorists, mainstream environmentalists risk bringing their entire movement into disrepute. Thus it is time for mainstream environmental groups and their supporters in Congress to disassociate themselves from those who use violence in the name of the environment and to see that they are brought to justice.

The Roots of Ecoterrorism

In the early 1970s a lone environmental activist, identified only as "The Fox", engaged in a sustained campaign of eco-sabotage, also termed ecotage, against Chicago-area firms. For three years he committed acts ranging from vandalizing the offices of corporations to more serious and dangerous crimes such as plugging industrial drains and smokestacks. Around the same time, a group in Minnesota called the "Bolt Weevils" and one in Arizona called the "Ecoraiders" carried out similar activities.

A few years later, environmental activist Edward Abbey romanticized ecotage in his novel, *The Monkey Wrench Gang.* In this story, four people roam the West wreaking havoc, destroying power poles, railroad lines, billboards, and any other sign of civilization that mar the landscape.

The "Earth First!" Movement

In 1981, Dave Foreman, a former lobbyist for the Wilderness Society, founded "Earth First!" This group, Foreman admits, was formed "to inspire others to carry out activities straight from the pages of *The Monkey Wrench Gang,* even though Earth First!, we agreed, would itself be ostensibly law-abiding." Strictly speaking, Foreman calls "Earth First!" a movement rather than an organization; there are no membership lists or officers, for instance. But the group, with about 10,000 people receiving its newsletter, provides a focal point for those interested in destructive and violent forms of protest. "Earth First! as an organization does not support or condone illegal or violent activities" and runs a disclaimer in the newsletter. However, it adds: "what an individual does autonomously is his or her own business."

Details for Destruction. Yet Foreman joined environmental activist Bill Haywood to write *Ecodefense: A Field Guide to Monkeywrenching,* a book that has sold more than 10,000 copies. While purporting to be for "entertainment purposes only," its 311 pages offer detailed advice on how, illegally and violently, to sabotage attempts to develop land and other resources. It describes how to drive spikes into trees to shatter chainsaws and saw mill blades when these cut the trees and logs. This "tree spiking" can injure lumberjacks and mill workers severely. Road spikes are recommended to flatten tires. Methods for destroying roads, disabling construction equipment, and cutting down power lines are discussed. In one chapter, the authors explains that power lines "are highly vulnerable to monkeywrenching from individuals or small groups."

During the Earth First! demonstration at the Arches National Park in mid-1981, power lines in nearby Moab, Utah, were cut. Foreman said that Earth First! was not directly responsible for such acts, but he added that "other people in Earth First! have *done* things, not as Earth First! though. . .Earth First!, a group, is not going to do any monkeywrenching. But if people who get the Earth First! newsletter do, that's fine."

In a letter interview he went even further, arguing that monkeywrenching "is morally *required* as self-defense on the part of the Earth."

Deep Ecology

Underlying the activities of many members of Earth First! and probably most ecoterrorists is the ideology of "Deep Ecology", which places the protection of nature above the promotion of humankind. The principles of Deep Ecology were first enunciated in 1972 by Norwegian philosopher Arne Naess. California sociologist Bill Devall and philosopher George Sessions of Sierra College in California are among the more prominent American Deep Ecologists. Naess advocates "a long range, human reduction [in the world's population] through mild but tenacious political and economic measures. This will make possible, as a result of increased habitat, population growth for thousands of species which are now constrained by human pressures." According to environmentalist Alston Chase, a newspaper columnist and chairman of Yellowstone National Park Library and Museum Association, who does not support Naess's views, "poets, philosophers, economists, and physicists joined the ecologists in a search for a new beginning." Through what Chase describes as a "swirl of chaotic, primeval theorizing, patterns began to form, and themes resonated," particularly the notions that nature is sacred and everything within the universe in interconnected.

Sacred Wilderness. Though Deep Ecology may be a bit jumbled, it has influenced a number of environmental activists. In one interview Foreman attacked the "anthropocentric" or "human-centered" philosophy of the Western world, explaining that "wilderness has a right to exist for its *own* sake, and for the sake of the diversity of life forms it shelters; we shouldn't have to justify the existence of a wilderness area by saying, 'Well, it protects the watershed, and it's a nice place to backpack and hunt, and it's pretty.'"

In his view not only is the wilderness sacred, but ecotage is a necessary element of Deep Ecology. Monkeywrenching is "a form of worship toward the earth. It's really a very spiritual thing to go out and do."

The mindset of the most extreme of these ecoterrorists is evident from a letter to the editor in *Earth First!* newsletter.

> The only way to stop all the destruction of our home is to decrease the birth rate or increase the death rate of people. It does no good to kill a few selected folks. That is a retail operation. What we need is a wholesale operation. . .The simple expedient: biological warfare! Think about it. It fits. It is species specific. Bacteria are, and viruses tend to be, deadly to only one species. Only a very few of human pathogens are shared by other partners on our planet. Biological warfare will have no impact on other creatures, big or small, if we design it carefully.

Ecoterriorism: A Present Danger?

Foreman claims that "the fact is, there's *already* an awful lot of monkeywrenching going on. . .The Forest Service tries to keep it quiet, industry tries to keep it quiet, and I think there has even been an effort in the media to downplay the extent and effectiveness of monkeywrenching in America today" since reporting such activities "would only encourage similar acts by many more of the millions of Americans who are strongly against the rape of what's left of our wilderness."

Destruction of Property

Foreman himself was arrested last year for allegedly conspiring to sabotage a tower carrying electrical power lines to pumping stations of the Central Arizona water project. Three others were caught trying to topple one of the towers; they also are charged with conspiring to wreak similar sabotage of power lines to two different nuclear plants and a nuclear weapons production facility.

The sabotage of construction equipment in logging operations has become common in Washington State. Damage in the millions of dollars has been inflicted by breaking equipment, smashing gauges, stealing batteries, and destroying radiators.

No Public Good. Environmental destruction certainly should be the target of reformers. But this does not justify extremist tactics, civil disobedience, and violence. Nor does this justify ignoring the balance that must be struck between ecological concerns and economic development. It is neither humane nor does it serve the public good to shut businesses needlessly, to restrict the supply of housing by prohibiting construction of new homes, or to drive up the costs of energy by reducing electrical generating capacity. There are ways to protect the environment without paying those prices. Some of these ways include privatization and ending of federal development subsidies. Environmental policies must be designed around natural market forces which would deliver more ecological amenities at lower cost.

Conclusion

Americans want to preserve a clean world — to conserve their environment. Americans too want an economy that offers them increasing economic opportunities. How to balance these two goals all too often splits Washington between myopic conservationists and equally myopic developers. Out of this split come the ecoterrorists, who believe that anything short of complete victory for "the environment" is a moral as well as a practical disaster.

Their extremist philosophy is leading to a guerrilla movement that is destroying property and injuring the innocent and one day will kill innocent workers or park employees.

Special Responsibility. To prevent this, policymakers and particularly establishment environmental groups, must respond to the ecoterrorists by rebuilding the moral consensus against the use of violence. The environmental movement has a special responsibility. It must no longer tolerate, let alone encourage, the ecoteurs. In particular, environmental groups should publicize the fact that the ecoteurs' violence sabotages the legitimate environmental groups. These mainstream groups thus should speak out forcefully to encourage their members to distance themselves from violent and destructive activities.

If Deep Ecology is not challenged at the philosophical level, the number of environmentalists committed to ecotage is likely to grow. And as more people put the "rights" of nature before those of humans, the more likely it is that innocent people are going to be killed.

19 ECOLOGY AND HUMAN VALUES

DEEP ECOLOGY: PRESERVING THE NATURAL ORDER

Fritjof Capra

Fritjof Capra, physicist, systems theorist and author, is the founder of the Elmwood Institute in Berkeley, California, an international organization dedicated to nurturing new ecological visions and applying them to the solution of current problems. The Elmwood Institute is a membership organization with a quarterly newsletter.

Points to Consider:

1. Describe the paradigm that is now receding.

2. How is the new paradigm, *deep ecology* defined?

3. What is the meaning of *shallow ecology*?

4. Explain the meaning of "The Mechanistic World View".

5. Why can "green economics" help save the global environment?

Fritjof Capra, "Deep Ecology: A New Paradigm", *Earth Island Journal,* Fall, 1987.

Since the seventeenth century, the goal of science has been knowledge that can be used to control, manipulate, and exploit nature.

The paradigm that is now receding has dominated our culture for several hundred years, during which it has shaped our modern Western society and has significantly influenced the rest of the world. This paradigm consists of a number of ideas and values, among them the view of the universe as a mechanical system composed of elementary building blocks, the view of the human body as a machine, the view of life in society as a competitive struggle for existence, the belief in unlimited material progress to be achieved through economic and technological growth, and last but not least, the belief that a society in which the female is everywhere subsumed under the male is one that follows a basic law of nature. In recent decades, all of these assumptions have been found to be severely limited and in need of radical revision.

Deep Ecology

The newly emerging paradigm can be described in various ways. It may be called a holistic worldview, emphasizing the whole rather than the parts. It may also be called an ecological worldview, using the term "ecological" in the sense of deep ecology. The distinction between "shallow" and "deep" ecology was made in the early seventies by the philosopher Arne Naess and has now been widely accepted as a very useful terminology to refer to the major division within contemporary environmental thought.

Shallow ecology is anthropocentric. It views humans as above or outside of nature, as the source of all value, and ascribes only instrumental, or use value to nature. Deep ecology does not separate humans from the natural environment, nor does it separate anything else from it. It does not see the world as a collection of isolated objects but rather as a network of phenomena that are fundamentally interconnected and interdependent. Deep ecology recognizes the intrinsic values of all living beings and views humans as just one particular strand in the web of life.

The new ecological paradigm implies a corresponding ecologically oriented ethic. The ethical framework associated with the old paradigm is no longer adequate to deal with some of the major ethical problems of today, most of which involve threats to non-human forms of life. With nuclear weapons that threaten to wipe out all life on the planet, toxic substances that contaminate the environment on a large scale, new and unknown micro-organisms awaiting release into the environment without knowledge of the consequences, animals tortured in the name of consumer safety—with all these activities occurring, it seems most important to introduce ecologically oriented ethical standards into modern science and technology.

The reason why most of old-paradigm ethics cannot deal with these problems is that, like shallow ecology, it is anthropocentric. Thus the most important task for a new school of ethics will be to develop a non-anthropocentric theory of value, a theory that would confer inherent value on non-human forms of life.

Value and Nature

Ultimately, the recognition of value inherent in all living nature stems from the deep ecological awareness that nature and the self are one. This, however, is also the very core of spiritual awareness. Indeed, when the concept of the human spirit is understood as the mode of consciousness in which the individual feels connected to the cosmos as a whole, it becomes clear that ecological awareness is spiritual in its deepest essence and that the new ecological ethics is grounded in spirituality.

In view of the ultimate identity of deep ecological and spiritual awareness, it is not surprising that the emerging new vision of reality is consistent with the "perennial philosophy" of spiritual traditions, for example, with that of Eastern spiritual traditions, the spirituality of Christian mystics, or the philosophy and cosmology underlying the Native American traditions.

In our contemporary culture, the spiritual essence of the deep ecological vision seems to find an ideal expression in the feminist spirituality advocated within the women's movement. Feminist spirituality is grounded in the experience of the oneness of all living forms and of their cyclical rhythms of birth and death. It is thus profoundly ecological and is close to Native American spirituality, Taoism, and other life-affirming, Earth-oriented spiritual traditions.

To discuss further aspects and consequences of the current shift of paradigms, I shall first outline the old paradigm and its influence on science and society, and shall then describe some implications of the new ecological vision of reality.

The Mechanistic World View

The mechanistic world view was developed in the 17th century by Galileo, Descartes, Bacon, Newton, and several others. Descartes based his view of nature on the fundamental division into two separate, independent realms: mind and matter. The material universe, including the human organism, was a machine that could in principle be understood completely by analyzing it in terms of its smallest parts.

Descartes' central metaphor was the clockwork, which had reached a high degree of perfection at that time and was seen as the ultimate machine. Thus Descartes wrote about the human body:

> I consider the human body as a machine. My thought compares a sick man and an ill-made clock with my idea of a healthy man and a well-made clock.

The enthusiasm of Descartes and his contemporaries for the metaphor of the body as a clock has an interesting parallel in the enthusiasm of many people today for the metaphor of the human brain as a computer. . .

As humans, we face problems that even the most sophisticated machines will never be able to handle, and our ways of thinking and communicating are totally different from those of a computer. Therefore, we have to draw a clear distinction between human intelligence and machine intelligence. Human intelligence, human judgments, human memory, and human decision are never completely rational, but are always colored by emotions. . .

Domination and Control

The mechanistic, fragmented approach is one basic characteristic of the old worldview. Another is the obsession with domination and control. In our society, political and economic power is exerted by the corporate elite. Our science and technology are based on the belief that an understanding of nature implies domination of nature by man. I use the word "man" here on purpose, because I am talking about a very important connection between the mechanistic worldview in science and the patriarchal value system, the male tendency of wanting to control everything.

In the history of Western science and philosophy, this connection occurred in the seventeenth century. Before the scientific revolution of Galileo, Descartes, Bacon, and Newton, the goals of science were wisdom, understanding of the natural order, and living in harmony with that order. Since the seventeenth century, the goal of science has been knowledge that can be used to control, manipulate, and exploit nature. Today both science and technology are used predominantly for purposes that are dangerous, harmful, and profoundly anti-ecological. . .

Green Economics

The application of system concepts to describe economic processes and activities is particularly urgent because virtually all our current economic problems are systemic problems that can no longer be understood through the fragmented approaches. . .

The aim of the new economic thinking, as of conventional economics, is to further economic development. However, this concept is given a different meaning. Instead of being defined as maximization of production and consumption, it is defined as maximization of human welfare. Human welfare has to do with health and human needs; with mental, emotional, and spiritual matters; with social and environmental issues.

New Values

Since many aspects of such a qualitative concept of economic development cannot be given monetary values, they will have to be implemented through the political process. The non-monetary choices to be made are political choices based on values. And this brings us to a most important aspect of the current paradigm shift, the question of values.

The shift to a new worldview and a new mode of thinking goes hand in hand with a profound change in values. What is so fascinating about these changes, to me, is a striking connection between the change of thinking and the change of values. Both can be seen as a shift from self-assertion to integration. As far as thinking is concerned, we can observe a shift from the rational to the intuitive, from analysis to synthesis, from reduction to holism, from linear to nonlinear thinking. I want to emphasize that the aim is not to replace one mode with the other, but rather to shift from the over-emphasis on one mode to a greater balance between the two.

As far as values are concerned, we observe a corresponding shift from expansion to conservation, from quantity to quality, from competition to cooperation, from domination and control to nonviolence.

RECOGNIZING AUTHOR'S POINT OF VIEW

This activity may be used as an individualized study guide for students in libraries and resource centers or as a discussion catalyst in small group and classroom discussions.

The capacity to recognize an author's point of view is an essential reading skill. Many readers do not make clear distinctions between descriptive articles that relate factual information and articles that express a point of view. Think about the readings in Chapter Three. Are these readings essentially descriptive articles that relate factual information or articles that attempt to persuade through editorial commentary and analysis?

Guidelines

1. The following are brief descriptions of sources that appeared in Chapter Three. Choose one of the following source descriptions that best defines each source in Chapter Three.

   Source Descriptions
   a. Essentially an article that relates factual information
   b. Essentially an article that expresses editorial points of view
   c. Both of the above
   d. Neither of the above

   ### Sources in Chapter Three

   • Source Fourteen: "Growth Is Killing the Environment"
   Murray Bookchin

   • Source Fifteen: "Economic Growth Is the Solution"
   Gro Harlem Brundtland

- Source Sixteen: "The Environmental Elite's Attack on Free Enterprise"
  Capital Research Center

- Source Seventeen: "Accounting for a Healthy Environment"
  James Robertson

- Source Eighteen: "Deep Ecology and Ecoterrorism Threaten Our Future"
  Doug Bandow

- Source Nineteen: "Deep Ecology: Preserving the Natural Order"
  Fritjof Capra

2. Summarize the author's point of view in one to three sentences for each of the readings in Chapter Three.

3. After careful consideration, pick out one reading that you think is the most reliable source. Be prepared to explain the reasons for your choice in a general class discussion.

CHAPTER 4

GLOBAL CLIMATE AND POOR NATIONS

20. SAVING THE ENVIRONMENT IN POOR   119
    NATIONS

    Richard E. Bissell

21. ENCOURAGING ENVIRONMENTAL   125
    DEVASTATION

    Brent Blackwelder

22. PROMOTING SUSTAINABLE   131
    DEVELOPMENT: A WORLD BANK
    PERSPECTIVE

    Jeremy Warford and Zeinab Partow

23. ECOLOGY AND DEVELOPMENT: 135
    A PERSPECTIVE FROM
    THIRD WORLD WOMEN

    Women's Resource Center, Philippines

20 GLOBAL CLIMATE AND POOR NATIONS

SAVING THE ENVIRONMENT IN POOR NATIONS

Richard E. Bissell

Richard Bissell made the following statement in his capacity as the Assistant Administrator for Policy and Program Coordination at the Agency for International Development (AID).

Points to Consider:

1. Identify the effects of climate change on developing nations.

2. Why would poor nations be hurt the worst by climate change?

3. What gases and human activities are most responsible for the greenhouse effect?

4. How does the Agency for International Development (AID) help poor nations with energy conservation?

5. What help does AID give to prevent the problem of deforestation?

Excerpted from testimony by Richard E. Bissell before the Senate Committee on Agriculture, Nutrition and Forestry, May 10, 1989.

AID has embarked on a number of activities to encourage multilateral development banks and other international agencies to support environmentally sound energy activities and to encourage new forestry activities.

Developed and developing countries alike clearly must take steps to create long term strategies to respond to potential climate change. The U.S. Agency for International Development is now working with other federal agencies, host governments, and a number of international organizations to understand and address these problems. . .

Effects of Climate Change

While clearly the threat of climate change is of concern to all countries, the potential effects of global climate change — such as sea level rise, changes in weather and rainfall patterns and the distribution of forests and productive agricultural lands — are likely to have far more serious consequences for people living in the developing world than for us.

It is obvious that developing countries which are already operating at the margin, with barely adequate food, health care, or shelter, would have great difficulty making the adjustments necessary to cope with major changes in agricultural patterns, forest cover, water resources and quality of life. These countries simply do not have the financial, technical, or natural resources to absorb the effects of such changes. Consequently, it is imperative that all countries take steps to mitigate the process of climate change.

Greenhouse Effect

Current scientific evidence suggests that four gases are primarily responsible for the greenhouse effect — carbon dioxide (49%), methane (18%), halocarbons (14%), and nitrous oxide (6%). Carbon dioxide is by far the most abundant of these gases and the single most important greenhouse gas. Fossil fuel combustion and deforestation are the most important man-made sources. The predominant sources of fossil fuel emissions are powerplants, industries, motor vehicles, and residential and commercial establishments.

AID is currently involved in a number of activities related to global warming. For example, they are funding studies to better understand the current and potential contribution of developing countries to changing levels of greenhouse gases and the effects of potential climate change on selected developing countries. . .

Moving toward eclipse

Energy Conservation

Higher levels of energy use explain the far greater contribution of the developed countries to global climate changes. Statistics on carbon dioxide emissions from fossil fuels show that the U.S. contributes about 25 percent of total emissions which arise primarily from fuels burned in motor vehicles and in the generation of electricity. Western Europe and Japan contribute about 23 percent with the Soviet Union and China contributing another 33 percent.

AID assisted countries combined currently contribute less than 10 percent of total fossil fuel emissions. However, when combined with the emissions from the newly-industrializing countries, China, and other non-AID assisted countries, the total contribution of developing countries accounts for about 25 percent of industrial carbon dioxide emissions and 40 percent of total greenhouse gas emissions — carbon dioxide, methane, halocarbons, and nitrous oxides.

The economic growth needed so badly by developing countries will require substantial increases in energy use. . .

AID has worked closely with many developing countries to promote energy efficiency, to substitute renewable energy resources for fossil fuels and to encourage the use of natural gas and improved power generation technologies, all of which help to reduce rates of increase in CO_2 emissions. . .

AID-assisted countries must have increasing supplies of energy if they are to develop. Some of these supplies can come from improvements in energy efficiency and the increasing use of renewable resources — hydro-electricity, biomass, solar, wind and geothermal. However, for the foreseeable future there will still be a need to use fossil fuel resources. AID can play a critical role, in helping developing countries to use the most environmentally sound technologies and to make use of those energy resources that are the least environmentally harmful. . .

Forestry

AID also supports a wide variety of efforts designed to reduce the rate of deforestation. These include activities to protect natural forests for sustained use, reforestation of degraded lands, and agroforestry programs to improve agricultural yields. Research activities focused on improved multipurpose tree species hold great promise for strengthening reforestation and agroforestry efforts. During fiscal year 1987, AID funded 146 forestry projects in 46 developing countries. The total amount of project funding for these activities was almost $600 million.

Forests and other vegetative cover benefit the environment by producing oxygen, fixing carbon, and modifying temperatures. In many tropical countries, and in some temperate countries as well, deforestation is occurring at an increasing rate in response to the pressures of population on marginal lands, the clearing of land for agriculture and cattle grazing, increased timber production, and demands for fuelwood. The proportion of increased atmospheric CO_2 attributed to deforestation is now estimated at 25 percent, adding significantly to the levels of CO_2 arising from the burning of fossil fuels.

AID recognizes forest resources can only be sustained through improved management of existing forests, reforestation, and afforestation. Today, only a very small percentage of the world's tropical forests are managed. The reasons are the lack of political commitment in the face of pressure to convert these lands to farm and pasture, the misleading perception that economic returns from alternative land uses are higher and limited experience in forest management. AID is actively supporting a number of programs to develop management strategies for natural forests and to change government policies which encourage slash and burn agriculture and environmentally harmful timber operations, colonization schemes, and cattle ranching in tropical forest areas.

Donor Coordination in Energy and Forestry

AID has embarked on a number of activities to encourage other bilateral agencies as well as the multilateral development banks and other international agencies to support environmentally sound energy activities and to encourage new forestry activities. . .

These efforts will focus not only on important local environmental and natural resource issues but also on issues such as responses to potential climate change and ozone depletion. . .

During the past year, AID has organized a collaborative group currently comprising the multilateral development banks (MDBs). The group expects to develop innovative approaches to meeting the financial and technical needs of developing country utilities, stressing the need to consider environmental effects. One of their first projects is the preparation of the guidebook on sound environmental management in the power sector for use by senior officials in the banks and in developing countries. We are also working with the U.S. Treasury to develop guidelines for use in reviewing energy projects proposed for funding by the multilateral development banks.

AID has participated actively in the development of the global Tropical Forest Action Plan and is working with other donors and host country governments to assess forest resources and needed management activities in more than 60 countries.

To summarize:

- AID-assisted countries contribute only a small fraction of global carbon dioxide emissions from fossil fuels and even with rapid economic growth this will be true.

- Promoting energy efficiency is an important component of our efforts in developing countries, but new energy sources will still be needed, both conventional and renewable.

- Deforestation contributes to global climate change, and AID in conjunction with other donors and developing countries is supporting efforts to reduce current rates of deforestation and to promote reforestation.

- Donor coordination and collaboration is necessary if we are to help developing countries limit emissions of greenhouse gases and cope with the effects of potential climate change. It is essential, however, that the U.S. take a lead role in showing other developed and developing countries that it can make the transition to reduced levels of fossil energy use and reductions in emissions of all greenhouse gases.

21 GLOBAL CLIMATE AND POOR NATIONS

ENCOURAGING
ENVIRONMENTAL
DEVASTATION

Brent Blackwelder

Brent Blackwelder is Vice-President of the Environmental Policy Institute, Friends of the Earth and the Oceanic Society. This statement was prepared by members of their International Department, including James Barnes (Senior Attorney), Chip Gay (Director of the Asian Development Bank Monitoring Project) and Bonnie Souza (Director of the Central American Project). Earlier this year the Environmental Policy Institute, Friends of the Earth and the Oceanic Society merged to form the new global advocacy organization with 33 international affiliates.

Points to Consider:

1. Why has U.S. foreign aid to Central America promoted environmental degradation?

2. Why has this aid promoted more poverty and suffering?

3. In specific ways, how have the rich benefited from aid programs?

4. How has U.S. military spending increased the environmental problems in Central America?

Excerpted from testimony by Brent Blackwelder before the Senate Committee on Agriculture, Nutrition and Forestry and the Committee on Appropriations, May 10, 1989.

Highly skewed land ownership and land use practices supported by the U.S. are largely responsible for the displacement of hundreds of thousands of people.

Central America

Citizens, policymakers and the press in the United States debate the social causes and consequences of conflict in Central America, but seldom address the profound environmental crisis now affecting the region. The U.S. has spent billions of dollars in Central America since 1981 to pursue its policies in the region. It is our contention that this economic and military assistance has contributed to severe environmental degradation in Central America.

Economic Assistance

U.S. development policies, which greatly favor the export sector, have supported IMF-like structural changes, the devotion of the best land and resources in Central America to cash crops for export, and the consequent migration of the region's majority—the subsistence sector—onto marginal lands, into the rain forest, or into the cities in search of employment. We believe that such an export-oriented model is a very dangerous one and is a prime way to decrease self-reliance. We are vigorously opposed to leading Central America down such a path with tragic environmental consequences. Highly skewed land ownership and land use practices supported by the U.S. are largely responsible for the displacement of hundreds of thousands of people, which has created vast numbers of internally-displaced refugees and placed serious pressures on the region's natural resources.

A good example is El Salvador, whose environment is the most degraded in Latin America. In El Salvador, less than 2 percent of the population controls nearly all the fertile land and 60 percent of the entire national territory. The National Parks Service reports that more than 95 percent of El Salvador's original tropical deciduous forests is gone and today less than 7 percent of the country is forested. US Agency for International Development (USAID) has reported that 494,000 acres of land currently in subsistence food production (roughly 10 percent of total area in El Salvador) need alternative, more ecologically-sound uses. Land held idle or in pasture by large growers should go into sustainable production for basic food crops to meet human needs, allowing marginal lands to be restored. Massive reforestation efforts are warranted, not only in El Salvador, but in all Central American countries, and USAID should devote the funds necessary to replant these forests.

In the Choluteca/Valle region in southwestern Honduras,

Cartoon by Blashko in People's Daily World

deforestation, primarily due to cotton production and cattle ranching which began in the 1950s, has rendered this part of Honduras a desert, resulting in severe erosion, summer droughts and winter floods. Due to desertification of this region, many thousands of Hondurans have been forced to colonize forested areas in other parts of the country, such as in Olancho.

Mangrove destruction in the gulf of Fonseca is a growing concern and a serious environmental issue that must be addressed in U.S. development policy. Our staff recently visited the region and reported that mangrove destruction is rapidly increasing as a result of increased commercial shrimp production, the production of non-traditional exports such as melons, salt processing, and tanneries. In the Gulf of Fonseca, 5,000 people in twelve communities have formed a new organization, The Committee for the Defense of the Flora and Fauna of the Gulf of Fonseca to defend the natural resources in the Gulf. These small fishermen, agriculturists and aquaculturists say that mangrove destruction is eliminating their way of life, that it is destroying the social structure for the people of southwestern Honduras who have lived off the mangroves for many generations. Production of cotton and non-traditional crops such as melons require excessive use of pesticides, which are poisoning the water, mollusks in the Gulf, and the bees necessary for pollination. Although alternative solar methods are being used to process salt, many processors are burning wood from the mangroves for this purpose.

Security Assistance

U.S. military spending in Central America has exacerbated the region's environment through a variety of ways. In El Salvador, the war's effects on the environment are deepening the country's ecological crisis and fueling the poverty behind the conflict. Wide areas of Morazan and northern Chalatenango provinces—areas of strongest guerrilla support and the worst fighting—have become virtual wastelands, with crops destroyed, forests burned and the landscape scarred with bomb craters. Counterinsurgency tactics that include defoliation, bombings and burning of forests have affected El Salvador, Guatemala, and Nicaragua. The contra war has been responsible for the kidnap or murder of over 75 environmental and natural resources employees in Nicaragua, the burning of reforestation projects, and continues to contribute to the increased deforestation rate in Honduras, especially along the Nicaraguan border. The contras are reported to be equipped with chainsaws which they are using without regulation to fell trees and clear land. According to the *Miami Herald,* they are receiving chainsaw safety training paid for by USAID. U.S. military spending in Honduras has greatly increased the deforestation rate, due to nearly continuous U.S. military operations, National Guard exercises and U.S. Army construction projects that have left the country criss-crossed with military roads and scarred with over ten major military bases and airstrips.

War in Central America has displaced hundreds of thousands, creating refugee populations in every Central American country which, in turn, places enormous additional pressure on the region's fragile tropical ecosystems. War has also forced Central American governments to divert monies away from environmental restoration and protection and into the military, resulting in a serious decline in environmental resource agencies and their budgets. Instead of addressing the severely-degraded condition of Central America's environment and the great need for building environmental institutions, the United States has devoted much of its bi-lateral assistance to military uses. For example, in 1986, the U.S. spent 18 times as much on military aid to El Salvador and Honduras as it did on environmental protection for the entire Caribbean region.

Alternative Policy Options

It is our perception that funding used to "promote security and stability" is leading directly to serious environmental damage and social upheaval that will guarantee continued social unrest and instability. We wish to suggest an innovative proposal which might help reverse the rapid decline in tropical forests and other natural resources on which ultimately the lives of all Central Americans depend. We believe international parks and nature reserves can help promote peace and enrivonmentally sound development in Central America by requiring a cooperative effort between neighboring nations. These zones could become centers of internationally significant research and economic development through rational resource management.

Conclusion

We also want to introduce to the Committee a booklet on sustainable development that we co-authored last year, entitled *Bankrolling Success: A Portfolio of Sustainable Projects.* We ask that it be incorporated into the record as an exhibit to our formal statement. In this context, we challenge the World Bank and the other MDBs to put the principles of truly sustainable development to work. "Sustainable Development" has become a phrase used widely by many institutions and organizations, which sets out a goal. It can, however, mean many different things.

This booklet sets out an intellectual framework for sustainability that is based on experience at the grass roots level in Latin America, Africa and Asia. The projects' features are, for the most part, sponsored by non-governmental organizations. They are not mega-projects, but rather are appropriate to the needs of the local people and draw on those people. The time frame of "success" is critical; one must look at the record over a period of decades rather than a rate of return figure derived from only a few years' experience.

22 GLOBAL CLIMATE AND POOR NATIONS

PROMOTING SUSTAINABLE DEVELOPMENT: A WORLD BANK PERSPECTIVE

Jeremy Warford and Zeinab Partow

Jeremy Warford, a British subject, holds a PhD in economics from the University of Manchester. He joined the World Bank staff in 1970, and is currently Senior Advisor in the Environmental Department.

Zeinab Partow from Iraq, is a researcher in the World Bank's Environment Department. She has a Master's degree in city and regional planning from the University of California at Berkeley.

Points to Consider:

1. How have world environmental problems changed?

2. Why has the World Bank changed its environmental policies?

3. Identify the World Bank's new policies.

4. What are the Bank's "environmental action plans"?

5. Why do environmental problems involve political conflicts of interests?

Jeremy Warford and Zeinab Partow "Evolution of the World Bank's Environmental Policy," *Finance and Development,* December 1989, pp. 5-8.

The Bank will attempt to ensure that its projects satisfy the often mutually supportive objectives of economic growth, poverty alleviation, and environmental protection.

In recent years, environmental degradation has become a matter of central concern for both developing and industrialized countries. The evidence is increasing that sound environmental management—far from being a luxury—is an essential ingredient for maintaining the natural resource base upon which most nations depend for their continued economic development. Developing nations will have to find a path to growth that differs markedly from the one traversed by their predecessors. And the industrialized ones will have to modify their behavior, curbing excessive use of resources and managing waste more efficiently.

Changing Problem

In developed and developing nations alike, governments have been increasingly investing in conservation measures (such as watershed protection and reforestation schemes), building ameliorative components into projects (such as pollution control equipment), strengthening environmental institutions, and introducing appropriate regulatory or legislative mechanisms. The World Bank has long stood committed to help in this regard—the first environmental advisor was recruited in 1969, establishing an Office of Environmental Affairs shortly thereafter. The numerous projects have contained environmental objectives, even if not labelled as such. But the rapidly unfolding events of the past two decades have called for a substantially greater attention to environmental matters and a more comprehensive approach than had been previously pursued by the Bank, as public discussion of these subjects has grown louder. In particular, a number of Bank lending operations, such as the Polonoroeste project in Brazil, the Botswana Livestock project, and the Indonesia Transmigration project, have been the subject of intense public criticism.

In 1987, in part spurred by this criticism, the Bank sharply adjusted its policies so as to favor environmental management. Underlying this change was the growing evidence and conviction that environmental degradation in its many forms constitutes a threat to economic development and growth. . .

The Bank is now convinced that the pervasive nature of environmental problems dictates a new approach: integrating environmental management into economic policymaking at all levels of government, supplementing the traditional project-by-project approach. The Bank also recognizes that special attention needs to be given to designing economic incentives in such a way that they induce environmentally sound practices, and experience shows that the two can be mutually supportive. Over the past two years, the Bank has made substantial progress on many fronts, particularly in the area of project lending. But much remains to be done, especially when it comes to country and sector work.

Country Environmental Studies

The Bank's new policy—making environmental issues part and parcel of the way that all staff view their work—is being implemented through a series of activities. The first step typically is a set of environmental studies, the most basic being environmental issues papers. These internal discussion documents, which have now been prepared for most active borrowing countries, identify key environmental problems and their underlying causes. . .

For some countries, the next conceptual step is the preparation of environmental action plans, which are undertaken by governments with broad local participation and international support. These plans cover a wide spectrum of activities, providing a framework for integrating environmental considerations into a nation's economic and social development program. Already the Bank is finding that these plans can be effective in helping government decisionmakers and donors set national priorities for environmental action. In addition, they help raise public awareness and can serve to strengthen policy formulation on many critical issues—for example, population, land, forest, and water management, and related fiscal matters.

In the case of some larger countries, or where important and complex problems arise in a country, greater selectivity and more in-depth treatment of issues may be required. Examples of such efforts include major studies in Indonesia, Nepal, and the Philippines, all of which focus on the multiple causes of deforestation and poor watershed management. A Bank study of the underlying causes of tropical deforestation in Brazil—which built upon previous work by the Brazilian government—provides a classic example of the way in which economic analysis can be used to identify appropriate environmental policies.

In still other cases, it makes most sense to address issues at a regional level, involving a number of countries. This is especially true where a resource or resource base occupies central importance in more than one country, where actions in one country may significantly affect another due to a shared resource, or where geographic realities necessitate the resolution of problems over a wide area. . .

Political Constraints

Even more fundamental causes of environmental problems

need attention, and inevitably involve politically sensitive questions about the distribution of land, income and wealth, and political and institutional power. Environmental problems inherently involve conflicts of interest: the upstream polluter damages downstream fisheries, mining or logging operations threaten indigenous tribes, deforestation threatens the global climate, and urgent present-day needs threaten the well-being of future generations. In most cases, the powerful damage the weak, or those who have little say in the decision-making process. Strong political will is therefore required to overcome the constraints posed by vested interests. Against this background, governments, the Bank, and other external agencies no doubt will encounter increasing resistance in trying to deal with environmental concerns.

Conclusion

To promote sound environmental management, and ultimately, sustainable development, the Bank will attempt to ensure that its projects satisfy the often mutually supportive objectives of economic growth, poverty alleviation, and environmental protection. The traditional concern with the environmental consequences of individual projects will now be enhanced by more rigorous environmental assessment procedures. However, these efforts alone are not sufficient. They must be accompanied by the integration of the environment into other aspects of the Bank's activities—particularly country economic work—if real progress is to be made.

23 GLOBAL CLIMATE AND POOR NATIONS

ECOLOGY AND DEVELOPMENT: A PERSPECTIVE FROM THIRD WORLD WOMEN

Women's Resource Center, Philippines

The following statement by the Women's Resource Center in the Philippines was reprinted from Pax et Libertas, *a quarterly publication of the Women's International League for Peace and Justice.*

Points to Consider:

1. How have women served as liberators?

2. Who are among the most oppressed people in the world?

3. How do indigenous women sustain nature?

4. Why has capitalism undermined the natural order in developing nations?

5. How did the green revolution undermine sustainable agriculture?

Women's Resource Center, Philippines, "The Ecological Crisis and the Third World," *Pax et Libertas,* December, 1989, pp. 8-9.

The green revolution further undermined the roles played by nature, women and peasants in sustainable agriculture.

The conventional analysis of women and environment stresses women as victims of environmental degradation. They have to walk further for fuel and water because of deforestation. Their health deteriorates because they must carry heavy loads over long distances due to the increasing scarcity of food.

Central Role

While it is important to emphasize these points, it is more dynamic to focus on women's central role in the environmental movement. Indigenous women, who have been involved in struggles against the destruction of their ancestral lands, are speaking not only as victims but as liberators. Their knowledge and experience of the production and defense of life in the face of anti-nature, anti-women programs of governments, global institutions and vested interests should be the subject of study.

Peasant Women

Women who are peasants and those categorized as national minorities or indigenous peoples are among the most marginalized and oppressed people in the world. Their struggles for self-determination offer strength and hope to people everywhere. Indigenous peoples have a deep reverence for nature. They worship trees, forests, and rivers. In their religious and cultural rites they seek blessings from goddesses and gods for the protection of nature. They regard their territories as ancestral homelands, a concept which has historical, cultural and ecological implications. Defense of the ancestral homeland from the forces of destruction means not only defense of territory but also of a whole lifestyle.

Communities

In indigenous communities, women are the primary food producers. They consider nature a living force, a partner in the production of life-sustaining food. Their productivity depends entirely on the continuing capacity of nature to renew its forests, rivers, and soil. Their ecological consciousness should be sustained and emulated. Their agriculture relies on internally recycled resources which are provided by nature. Indigenous seed varieties, which have been selected, improved, conserved and propagated by women, provide the germ plasm that is still being used today, albeit to a lesser degree because these varieties are being hijacked by transnational corporations (TNCs) and agencies such as the International Rice Research Institute.

"Another sign of spring — the return of the lawn chemicals."

Illustration by Carol*Simpson

Capitalism

With the industrial revolution and capitalist development, subsistence economies which relied on nature, women, and peasants for the satisfaction of basic needs were transformed into a market economy dependent on commodity production to ensure the generation of profit. Colonization was necessary to guarantee the continuous supply of raw material and to develop markets to absorb the surplus products of capitalist countries.

In this framework, the wealth created by nature and women was rendered invisible. Economic growth and productivity came to be equated with the generation of cash, profit and surplus. In this model, nature, women, peasants, tribal peoples and communities whose work does not necessarily generate cash, profit and surplus are not regarded as creative of productive. They are simply considered resource bases, raw materials, manpower (sic!) and inputs.

Western Values

Development from the perspective of western experts and TNCs ensured the perpetuation of the economic and political domination of the developed nations over the Third World, over nature and over women. The "Green Revolution" or "scientific agriculture" hastened the erosion of subsistence economies. Cash crops took precedence over production for sustenance.

137

The green revolution further undermined the roles played by nature, women and peasants in sustainable agriculture. The control of seeds and crops and the access to land use, forests and waters shifted to TNCs, governments and international lending agencies. Renewable inputs from farms, forests and rivers were replaced by non-renewable inputs from TNCs producing fertilizer, pesticide, seeds and chemical animal feed. Man-made diversion dams replaced rivers as the source of irrigation water. Flooding, drought, topsoil erosion and desertification resulted from the implementation of development programs which violate the natural life cycle of rivers, soil, mountains and forests.

Transfer of Power

The management of food systems, forests and rivers shifted from peasants and women to food and agri-business TNCs, mining and logging corporations, and international lending institutions. Village men became low-paid lumberjacks; women were deprived of traditional land use rights. Forestry laws enacted by colonial and post-colonial governments to facilitate logging led to massive destruction of the forests. When indigenous people have defended their forests against such abuse, the military apparatus has been used to repress them.

Fighting Oppression

While the roles of Third World women and indigenous peoples in history remain invisible, women have been in the forefront of many of the struggles against the efforts of governments or TNCs to dislocate them from their beloved lands. The struggle against the World Bank-sponsored Chico River Dam project in the Cordillera region of the Philippines in the mid-1970s is one of many fine examples. Women trekked to the site of the surveyors' camp and dismantled their tents. They were detained in military barracks for their opposition, but they continued resisting until the World Bank and Philippine government were forced to cancel the whole project. Walden Bello described this in his book *Development Debacle* as one of the worst setbacks suffered by one of the most sophisticated international financial institutions. This defeat was organized by pre-industrial tribal peoples!

Common Ground

While the environmental, peace, and women's movements are gaining more adherents, efforts to co-opt these movements by governments and institutions such as the World Bank are becoming more sophisticated. By linking and identifying with the struggles of Third World women, activists in the First World will have the strength to resist moves of vested interests to co-opt them. The focus of movements working for radical change will be to find common ground, seeking strength from the struggles of the most marginalized and oppressed people in the world.

WHAT IS EDITORIAL BIAS?

This activity may be used as an individualized study guide for students in libraries and resource centers or as a discussion catalyst in small group and classroom discussions.

The capacity to recognize an author's point of view is an essential reading skill. The skill to read with insight and understanding involves the ability to detect different kinds of opinions or bias. Sex bias, race bias, ethnocentric bias, political bias and religious bias are five basic kinds of opinions expressed in editorials and all literature that attempts to persuade. They are briefly defined in the glossary below.

Glossary of Terms for Reading Skills

SEX BIAS—the expression of dislike for and/or feeling of superiority over the opposite sex or a particular sexual minority

RACE BIAS—the expression of dislike for and/or feeling of superiority over a racial group

ETHNOCENTRIC BIAS—the expression of a belief that one's own group, race, religion, culture or nation is superior. Ethnocentric persons judge others by their own standards and values

POLITICAL BIAS—the expression of political opinions and attitudes about domestic or foreign affairs

RELIGIOUS BIAS—the expression of a religious belief or attitude

Guidelines

1. From the readings in Chapter Four, locate five sentences that provide examples of editorial opinion or bias.

2. Write down each of the above sentences and determine what kind of bias each sentence represents. Is it *sex bias, race bias, ethnocentric bias, political bias or religious bias?*

3. Make up one sentence statements that would be an example of each of the following: *sex bias, race bias, ethnocentric bias, political bias and religious bias.*

4. See if you can locate five sentences that are factual statements from the readings in Chapter Four.

CHAPTER 5

PUBLIC POLICY AND CLIMATE CHANGE

24. THE POLITICS OF ECOLOGY: 143
     IDEAS IN CONFLICT
     Howard Hawkins

25. WHY WE ARE FAILING   150
     Barry Commoner

26. WHY WE ARE SUCCEEDING   156
     William A. Nitze

27. HUMAN VALUES IN A SUSTAINABLE   161
     WORLD
     *Lester R. Brown, Christopher Flavin
     and Sandra Postel*

28. FREE MARKET VALUES WILL PROTECT   168
     THE ENVIRONMENT
     Fred Smith

24 PUBLIC POLICY AND CLIMATE CHANGE

THE POLITICS OF ECOLOGY: IDEAS IN CONFLICT

Howard Hawkins

Howard Hawkins is a carpenter active in the Vermont Greens and the Left Green Network. This article is adapted from an article which originally appeared in the July/August 1989 issue of the Boston-based newsletter, Resist.

Points to Consider:

1. How is mainstream environmentalism different from populist ecology?

2. Compare social ecology with ecological marxism.

3. What is the difference between deep ecology and the Earth First! movement?

4. Explain the meaning of bioregionalism.

5. What is ecofeminism?

6. How do the New Age Greens, Progressive Greens and Left Greens differ from each other?

Adapted from an article which originally appeared in the July/August 1989 issue of the Boston-based newsletter *Resist*.

As popular movements grow in response to the mounting ecological crisis, exactly what the politics of ecology should be is becoming a matter of widespread contention. The environmentalism with which we have been familiar—a largely legalistic, lobbying, reform movement concerning a single issue in society—is rapidly evolving into ecology—a multi-issue movement for fundamental social change. . .

But exactly what this ecology should be is a matter of much debate. The different schools of thought have different answers.

Social ecology, bioregionalism, deep ecology, ecofeminism and ecological Marxism are the ideological schools offering answers to these questions in the radical ecology movement. Earth First!, the Green Committees of Correspondence and the Left Green Network are the principal U.S. groups that are trying to give the movement organized expression.

But to understand these schools of thought, we also need to understand mainstream environmentalism and what is the largest and fastest growing sector of environmental activism, populist environmentalism.

The Mainstream

Many activists in radical ecology movements today are radicalized by their frustration with mainstream environmentalism, epitomized by "The Group of Ten," including the National Wildlife Federation, the Sierra Club, the Natural Resources Defense Council and others. They are staff-based organizations with a large, but passive, mailing-list membership that supports the staff through donations. The staffs focus on lobbying and legal action.

Explicitly in the U.S. tradition of non-partisan pragmatic reform, the mainstream environmental groups descend directly from the conservation movement that emerged around the turn of the century and achieved the establishment of the first national parks.

These groups were also at the center of the second wave of environmentalism in the 1970s that won federal air and water legislation. Today they are calling for a "third-wave environmentalism" that employs market-based incentives for environmental protection. This idea of market-based incentives is the theme openly embraced by President Bush in his proposals for reducing air pollution.

Radical ecologists criticize mainstream environmentalism for making compromises with the establishment and for not recognizing that ecological destruction is not simply a result of mistakes or bad policy that can be corrected within the existing social framework, but is inherent in society as now constituted.

DOESN'T iT seem Like JUST yesTeRDAY THAT WE WERE WORRYING ABOUT HOW THE WORLD WOULD COPE WiTH NUCLEAR **WINTER**......

GREENHOUSE EFFECT

Reprinted with permission of *Star Tribune*.

Populist Environmentalism

This type of environmental activism stresses street mobilizations as well as lobbying. Staff work is focused on community organizing and developing grass-roots leadership. The major national organizations in this trend, including the Citizens' Clearinghouse on Hazardous Waste and the National Toxics Campaign, are coalitions of grass-roots groups.

The populist environmentalism may be the fastest growing grass-roots movement in the country. It ranges from the struggles of Black and Latino communities in Los Angeles to prevent the siting of trash incinerators in their neighborhoods, to Vermonters Organized for a Clean-up fighting toxic waste sites statewide, and Black church people in Warren County, North Carolina, organizing civil disobedience to block a PCB dump. There are literally hundreds of these grass-roots groups fighting the polluters in all regions of the country. . .

The populist trend is broad because it enables people to respond to immediate problems in their communities. It also encompasses a class and racial diversity that neither mainstream environmental groups nor the more ideological ecology trends have even approached. . .

Ecological Marxism

Rather than critically and selectively incorporating particular aspects of Marx's critique of capitalism into an ecological perspective, these theorists want to add an ecological aspect to their theory of capitalist economic crisis.

Andre Gorz has tried to add ecological aspects to a neo-Marxist view that is oriented toward the new social movements rather than the traditional working class. Jim O'Connor is also addressing environmental issues within a Marxist framework, but with more emphasis on the working class as agents of social transformation.

Ecological Marxism has no organized expression, however, other than the new journal, *Capitalism, Nature, and Socialism*, that O'Connor and his colleagues have started.

Social Ecology

Among the various ideologies in the radical ecology movement that are trying to offer a comprehensive social analysis and program of change, social ecology is the oldest form. This ecological perspective can be traced to Murray Bookchin's 1964 essay "Ecology and Revolutionary Thought," where the radically anti-capitalist and anti-hierarchical implications of an ecological perspective were first advanced.

Social ecology's basic thesis is that the ecological crisis, the attempt to dominate nature, stems from the domination of human by human. Therefore, goes the argument, the reharmonization of humanity with nature presupposes a reharmonization between humans. This analysis yields a vision of non-hierarchical confederacy – a stateless, decentralized, democratic society based on communal ownership of the means of production.

Deep Ecology

Deep ecology is a term coined by the Norwegian philosopher Arne Naess, in a 1973 essay. At one level it simply means that an ecological outlook has profound social implications. It is at this level that most activists who claim to subscribe to the theory understand it.

Academic deep ecology, as developed by Naess and his U.S. proteges Bill Devall and George Sessions, is premised on two ultimate norms: self-realization for every being and a "biocentric" equality among species. How to reconcile the self-realization of smallpox viruses and that of their human hosts, and whether "human interference" in the form of vaccinations is permissible, is the kind of how-many-angels-on-a-pinhead debates one finds in academic deep ecology.

In an attempt to reach outside academia, Naess and Sessions

have enumerated an eight-point "platform" of deep ecology. In it they argue for reducing human population, reducing human interference in the non-human world and reducing human standards of living.

But the platform contains no theory of the state, capitalism, cultural and technological evolution or the social roots of population dynamics. In practice, academic deep ecologists tend to preach Malthusian doom about population, condemn "industrialism" and moralize about the evils of "consumerism".

Grass-roots "deep ecologists" tend to be lifestyle and spiritually oriented, with those in Earth First! also involved in civil disobedience and sabotage in defense of wild areas.

Earth First!

Earth First! was initiated by conservationists who were frustrated with the compromising deals made by the mainstream environmentalists. Earth First! has no formal structure of accountability, which allows its de facto leadership around the journal *Earth First!* to set the ideological tone for the movement.

The leadership claims adherence to deep ecology, with a particular emphasis on a Malthusian view on population questions. *Earth First!* has carried articles praising AIDS as a form of population control.

Dave Foreman, publisher of *Earth First!*, has called for closing off immigration from Mexico to protect the U.S. wilderness (as if Mexicans, not corporate developers, are strip mining, clear cutting and strip developing). He argues too for "letting nature take its course," for example, by letting Ethiopians starve instead of sending them food. . .

Bioregionalism

Bioregionalism is the idea that human societies should be decentralized and oriented economically and politically toward an ecological adaptation to the unique qualities of natural biogeographical regions. The idea was originally popularized by *CoEvolution Quarterly* from the mid-1970s on, after the publication of ecologist Raymond Dassman's essay on "Biogeographical Provinces" in 1976, and subsequent commentary on the political implications of this ecological concept.

Bioregional activism tends to focus on personal lifestyle change and alternative projects, often with a spiritual overtone of reverence for the Earth.

As such, it is more subculture trying to repair rather than confronting the existing system and trying to transform it. Social ecologists and Left Green argue that bioregionalism cannot achieve its goal unless it challenges capitalism as a centralizing growth-oriented system.

Ecofeminism

Ecofeminism shares with social ecology the understanding that social domination and the attempt to dominate nature are related. Within this, it stresses the role that the women's movement can play in bringing about peace and ecological harmony.

As an activist movement, it flowered in the late 1970s and early 1980s as women in the anti-nuclear alliances formed their own affinity groups and organized their own actions, including the Women's Pentagon Actions.

In recent years, while organized ecofeminist activism has subsided, two ideological wings have emerged which are parallel to the deep/social ecological division in the larger ecology movement. One wing of ecofeminism is spiritually oriented, focused on personal transformation. The other, social ecofeminism, insists that ecofeminism needs to address economic and class issues both in theory and in collective action.

The Greens

If the radical ecology movement is going to address the roots of the ecological crisis, it is going to have to be integrated with social movements for peace, freedom and justice in a multi-issue movement for fundamental social change. Single-issue oriented radical ecology groups like Earth First! and the North American Bioregional Congress have their place. But among the organizations of the radical ecology movement, it is only the Greens who aspire to provide the multi-issue framework that is required.

The Green Committees of Correspondence (CoC) is a network of some 200 local Green groups across the United States. These groups are active in a wide variety of community struggles, alternative projects, public education and (usually independent) electoral politics.

There are currently three tendencies within the Greens. The New Age Greens battle "industrialism" rather than capitalism, and "consumerism" rather than decisions made at the point of production that determine the choices consumers have. . .

Progressive Greens are oriented toward left-liberal coalition politics and such organizations as the National Rainbow Coalition and the Democratic Socialists of America. Most adherents to those perspectives view "Green" as a metaphor for the environment, as one more issue to add to their programmatic laundry list, rather than as a comprehensive political outlook.

The Left Greens have organized a Left Green Network to advance their views within the Green movement, the left and the grass-roots movement. These views include independent politics, anti-capitalism and social ecology. The Left Green Network presently includes activists from a variety of left organizations in addition to the Greens, including the Socialist Party, Solidarity, the IWW (Wobblies) and the Catholic Worker movement. The network also includes many independent leftists looking for an organizational home.

25 PUBLIC POLICY AND CLIMATE CHANGE

WHY WE ARE FAILING

Barry Commoner

Barry Commoner is director of the Center for the Biology of Natural Systems, Queens College, City University of New York.

Points to Consider:

1. How much has the environment improved since 1970?

2. What are some examples of improvements in the environment?

3. Define the major failures of the environmental movement.

4. How have technological changes caused environmental problems?

5. Why is it impossible to protect the environment by controlling pollution?

Barry Commoner, "Why We Have Failed", *Greenpeace*, September/October, 1989.

The lesson is plain: pollution prevention works; pollution control does not.

In 1970, in response to growing concern, the U.S. Congress began a massive effort to undo the pollution damage of the preceding decades. In short order, legislators in Washington passed the National Environmental Protection Act (NEPA) and created the Environmental Protection Agency (EPA) to administer it. These two events are the cornerstone of what is indisputably the world's most vigorous pollution control effort, a model for other nations and a template for dozens of laws and amendments passed since. Now, nearly 20 years later, it is time to ask an important and perhaps embarrassing question: how far have we progressed toward the goal of restoring the quality of the environment?

The answer is indeed humbling. Apart from a few notable exceptions, environmental quality has improved only slightly, and in some cases worsened. Since 1975, emissions of sulfur dioxide and carbon monoxide are down by about 19 percent, but nitrogen oxides are up about 4 percent. Overall improvement in major pollutants amounts to only about 15 to 20 percent, and the rate of improvement has actually slowed considerably.

The Exceptions

There are several notable and heartening exceptions. Pollution levels of a few chemicals—DDT and PCBs in wildlife and people, mercury in the fish of the Great Lakes, strontium 90 in the food chain and phosphate pollution in some local rivers—have been reduced by 70 percent or more. Levels of airborne lead have declined more than 90 percent since 1975.

The successes explain what works and what does not. Every success on the very short list of significant environmental quality improvements reflects the same remedial action: production of the pollutant has been stopped. DDT and PCB levels have dropped because their production and use have been banned. Mercury is much less prevalent because it is no longer used to manufacture chlorine. Lead has been taken out of gasoline, and strontium has decayed to low levels because the United States and the Soviet Union had the good sense to stop the atmospheric nuclear bomb tests that produced it.

The lesson is plain: pollution prevention works; pollution control does not. Only where production technology has been changed to eliminate the pollutant has the environment been substantially improved. Where it remains unchanged, where an attempt is made to trap the pollutant in an appended control device—the automobile's catalytic converter or the power plant's scrubber—environmental improvement is modest or nil. When a pollutant is attacked at the point of origin, it can be eliminated. But once it is produced, it is too late.

Progress and Pollution

Most of our environmental problems are the inevitable result of the sweeping technological changes that transformed the U.S. economic system after World War II: the large, high-powered cars; the shift from fuel-efficient railroads to gas-guzzling trucks and cars; the substitution of fertilizers for manure and crop rotation and of toxic synthetic pesticides for ladybugs and birds.

By 1970, it was clear that these technological changes were the root cause of environmental pollution. But the environmental laws now in place do not address the technological origin of pollutants. I remember the incredulity in Senator Muskie's voice during NEPA hearings when he asked me whether I was really testifying that the technology that generated postwar economic progress was also the cause of pollution. I was.

Because environmental legislation ignored the origin of the assault on environmental quality, it has dealt only with its subsequent problems—in effect defining the disease as a collection of symptoms. As a result, all environmental legislation mandates only palliative measures. The notion of preventing pollution—the only measure that really works—has yet to be given any administrative force.

The goal established by the Clean Air Act in 1970 could have been met if the EPA had confronted the auto industry with a demand for fundamental changes in engine design, changes that were practical and possible. And had American farmers been required to reduce the high rate of nitrogen fertilization, nitrate water pollution would now be falling instead of increasing.

If the railroads and mass transit were expanded, if the electric power system were decentralized and increasingly based on cogenerators and solar sources, if American homes were weatherized, fuel consumption and air pollution would be sharply reduced. If brewers were forbidden to put plastic nooses on six-packs of beer, if supermarkets were not allowed to wrap polyvinylchloride film around everything in sight, if McDonalds restaurants could rediscover the paper plate, if the use of plastics was cut back to those things considered worth the social costs (say, artificial hearts or video tape), then we could push back the petrochemical industry's toxic invasion of the biosphere.

Of course, all this is easier said than done. I am fully aware that what I am proposing is no small thing. It means that sweeping changes in the major systems of production agriculture, industry, power production and transportation would be undertaken for a social purpose: environmental improvement. This represents social (as contrasted with private) governance of

---

ASSAULTING THE ENVIRONMENT

We must recognize that the assault on the environment cannot be effectively controlled but must be prevented; that prevention requires transforming the structure of the technosphere, bringing it into harmony with the ecosphere; that this requires a fundamental redesign of the major industrial, agricultural and transportation systems; that such a transformation of the systems of production conflicts with the short-term profit-maximizing goals that govern investment decisions under capitalism; and that, accordingly, politically suitable means must be developed that bring the public interest in long-term environmental quality to bear upon these decisions. Finally, because the problem is global and deeply linked to the disparity between the development of the planet's Northern and Southern hemispheres, what we propose to do in the United States must be compatible with the global task of closing the economic gap between the rich North and the poor South—and indeed must facilitate it.

Barry Commoner, The Nation, *April 30, 1990*

---

the means of production—an idea that is so foreign to what passes for our national ideology that even to mention it violates a deep-seated taboo.

The major consequence of this powerful taboo is the failure to reach the goals in environmental quality that motivated the legislation of the 1970s.

Risk and Public Morality

In the absence of a prevention policy, the EPA adopted a convoluted pollution control process. First, the EPA must estimate the degree of harm represented by different levels of the numerous environmental pollutants. Next, some "acceptable" level of harm is chosen (for example, a cancer risk of one in a million) and emission and/or ambient concentration standards that can presumably achieve that risk level are established.

Polluters are then expected to respond by introducing control measures (such as automobile exhaust catalysts or power plant stack scrubbers) that will bring emissions to the required levels. If the regulation survives the inevitable challenges from industry (and in recent years from the administration itself), the polluters will invest in the appropriate control systems. Catalysts are attached to cars, and scrubbers to the power plants and trash-burning incinerators. If all goes well—and it frequently does not—at least some areas of the country and some production facilities are then in compliance with the regulation.

Acceptable Pollution Level

The net result is that an "acceptable" pollution level is frozen in place. Industry, having invested heavily in equipment designed to reach just the required level, is unlikely to invest in further improvements.

Clearly, this process is the opposite of the preventive approach to public health. It strives not for the continuous improvement of environmental health, but for the social acceptance of some, hopefully low, risk to health. By contrast, the preventive approach aims at progressively reducing the risk to health. It does not mandate some socially convenient stopping point. The medical professions, after all, did not decide that the smallpox prevention program could stop when the risk reached one in a million. They kept on, and the disease has now been wiped out worldwide.

The Real Solution

The fate of Alar, the pesticide used to enhance the marketability of apples, provides a recent instructive example of what prevention means. Like many other petrochemical products, Alar poses a health risk. It has been proven to induce cancer in test animals. As in many other such cases, a debate has flourished over the extent of the hazard to people, especially children, and over what standards should be applied to limit exposure to "acceptable" levels.

In June, Alar broke out of the pattern when the manufacturer, Uniroyal, decided that regardless of the toxicological uncertainties, Alar would be taken off the market. They acted simply because parents were unhappy about raising their children on apple juice that represented any threat to their health. Food after all, is supposed to be good for you.

This is a clear-cut example of the benefits of prevention, as opposed to control. Pollution prevention means identifying the source of the pollutant in the production process, eliminating it from that process and substituting a more environmentally benign method of production. This differentiates it from source reduction (reducing the amount of the pollutant produced, either through altering processes or simple housekeeping and pollution control.) Once a pollutant is eliminated, the elaborate system of risk assessment, standard setting and the inevitable debates and litigation become irrelevant.

Instituting the practice of prevention rather than control will require the courage to challenge the taboo against questioning the dominance of private interests over the public interest. But I suggest that we begin with an open public discussion of what has gone wrong, and why. That is the necessary first step on the road toward realizing the nation's unswerving goal—restoring the quality of the environment.

26 PUBLIC POLICY AND CLIMATE CHANGE

WHY WE ARE SUCCEEDING

William A. Nitze

William A. Nitze is the Deputy Assistant for the Environment at the United States Department of State.

Points to Consider:

1. What has been done by nations to help save the ozone layer?

2. How has the United States acted to protect the ozone layer?

3. What measures have been taken to deal with the global problems of hazardous waste?

4. Identify the steps that are being taken to deal with acid rain.

5. What actions are being taken to combat the problem of global warming?

Excerpted from testimony by William A. Nitze before the House Foreign Affairs Subcommittee on Human Rights and International Organizations, April 6, 1989.

The protocol provides for a 50 percent reduction in production and consumption of many ozone-depleting chemicals enforced by restrictions on trade in those substances containing them.

Environmental issues have risen to the top of the international policy agenda over the last few years. Spurred by rising public concern, leaders in many countries are pressing for more far reaching international cooperation with respect to the environment. For example, the governments of Britain, France and Italy have recently become far more active on international environmental issues than in the past. The Soviet Union has extended Glasnost and Perestroika into the environmental realms, publicly acknowledging environmental concerns in the U.S.S.R. and calling for greater bilateral and international cooperation on global environmental issues.

Protection of the Ozone Layer

The Montreal Protocol on substances that deplete the ozone layer was adopted in September 1987, ratified by the U.S. in April 1988, and entered into force January 1, 1989. The protocol provides for a 50 percent reduction in production and consumption of many ozone-depleting chemicals enforced by restrictions on trade in those substances containing them. U.S. support for the protocol was essential to reaching an effective agreement and earned the U.S. kudos for leadership on this important environmental issue.

On March 3, the President, in his remarks to the winners of the Westinghouse Science Talent Search at the National Academy of Science, expressed U.S. support for the complete elimination of ozone-depleting CFCs and halons by the year 2000 subject to the availability of safe substitutes. On March 5, EPA Administrator William Reilly in his opening statement at the London "Save the Ozone Layer" conference (called by Mrs. Thatcher, with more than 120 countries participating) announced that the United States will "strongly support an international phase-out of CFCs and halons."

The March 1988 Ozone Trends Panel report, the result of an 18-month effort by an international team of over 100 scientists led by NASA, indicated that ozone depletion may be worse than anticipated at the time of adoption of the Protocol. Industry has made progress in the development of alternative substances and technologies to ozone-depleting chlorofluorocarbons (CFCs) for use in refrigeration and air conditioning, electronics, foam-blowing and other applications. DuPont plans to phase-out production of fully halogenated CFCs by 2000 if substitutes are available in adequate supply, and other U.S. producers have indicated that they will join in the phase-out if there is

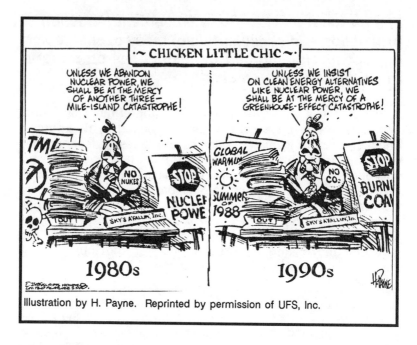

Illustration by H. Payne. Reprinted by permission of UFS, Inc.

international agreement to do so.

Hazardous Waste Exports

The U.S. has been a world leader in the management of hazardous wastes, being one of the first countries to institute controls over hazardous waste exports. These controls have been at least as stringent as controls in any other country. However, international dumping incidents and the possible growth in volume of waste exports have demonstrated a need to strengthen U.S. policy.

President Bush announced on March 10 that he will seek legislative authority to ban exports of hazardous wastes from the U.S. unless we have an agreement with the receiving country that provides for environmentally sound management of these wastes. Current domestic policy requires notice to and consent from the receiving country before a shipment can take place. Once those conditions have been met, however, the U.S. government does not have the authority to stop shipments which may pose unacceptable environmental risks. The new authority sought by the President will enable the U.S. to ban such exports except where shipment and disposal meet environmentally sound standards stipulated in agreements worked out between the U.S. and receiving countries. Such steps should reduce the risk of an international environmental incident caused by inappropriate management of the U.S.-origin hazardous waste in a recipient country.

The U.S. has also actively participated in negotiations over the last 18 months, under United Nations Environment Programme (UNEP) auspices, on a global convention to regulate transboundary movement of hazardous waste. Thirty-four countries — not including the U.S. and several of our European allies — signed the Convention when it was opened for signature on March 22.

The Administration is currently reviewing the convention to determine whether it serves our national interest to become a party. The Convention prohibits exports to and imports from non-parties except where a bilateral agreement exists specifying environmentally sound disposal. It also provides for notification to and written consent from importing and transit countries and prohibits hazardous and other waste exports or imports if there is reason to believe environmentally sound disposal will not take place. The convention's control measures extend to household waste and incinerated ash in addition to hazardous wastes.

Acid Rain

President Bush will soon propose legislation providing for significant reductions in U.S. CO_2 emissions and other acid rain precursors. The amendments to the Clean Air Act resulting from Congressional action in response to the President's proposal will set the domestic parameters within which we can then proceed to negotiate an air quality accord with Canada.

The Canadians made clear in the Ottawa meeting between the President and Prime Minister Mulroney, that they recognized and appreciated the positive and constructive approach being taken by this Administration. An accord with Canada could meet the key objectives of both countries once the U.S. has finalized its domestic approach to acid rain.

Global Climate Change

Projections indicate a 50 percent probability of global warming of 1.5 to 4.5 degrees centigrade by the year 2100. Climate changes resulting from warming of this magnitude would have consequences for every nation and every aspect of human activity. . .

The U.S. has taken the lead. It has organized the Intergovernmental Panel on Climate Change (IPCC), and we chair the Response Strategies Working Group (RSWG) of the IPCC. The IPCC is committed to an ambitious schedule of work leading up to a report to the Second World Climate Conference in the fall of 1990. RSWG's section of the report will discuss a menu of possible response strategies ranging from energy efficiency to reforestation and implementation mechanisms from market incentives to legal and institutional alternatives.

These issues, including calls by some countries for a climate convention, will be discussed in upcoming meetings of the U.N. Environment Program, the World Meteorological Organization and particularly the IPCC. We believe it is premature, however, to be considering a sweeping "law of the air" or supranational authorities to deal with climate change, as some have recently advocated. To help shape this process in a way consistent with its interests, the U.S. will have to develop an active international strategy for dealing with climate change which is in turn based on an evolving domestic strategy.

Overview

All nations face a new imperative. In a way, our global society of states is not unlike our early American state when in Benjamin Franklin's time honored words: "We must all hang together or, most assuredly, we shall all hang separately."

No country can deal with these environmental problems alone. They respect no boundaries. America has an opportunity to lead in building international cooperation. It will not be easy. But sooner or later, governments must see that only by joining with others will we be able to meet the global environmental challenges of the future.

27 PUBLIC POLICY AND CLIMATE CHANGE

HUMAN VALUES IN A SUSTAINABLE WORLD

Lester R. Brown, Christopher Flavin and Sandra Postel

Lester R. Brown is president of the Worldwatch Institute. Christopher Flavin and Sandra Postel are both vice presidents for research at the Institute.

Points to Consider:

1. How are the world's basic environmental problems described?

2. What is the meaning of an "environmentally sustainable society"?

3. Why is solar power important for a sustainable environment?

4. How will land use and agricultural practices change in a sustainable economy?

5. Why will basic values be different in a sustainable environment?

Lester R. Brown, Christopher Flavin and Sandra Postel, "Earth Day 2030", *World Watch,* March/April, 1990.

Because of the strain on resources it creates, materialism simply cannot survive the transition to a sustainable world.

Threats such as climate change and ozone depletion underscore the fact that ecological degradation has reached global proportions. Meanwhile, the increasing severity and spread of more localized problems—including soil erosion, deforestation, water scarcity, toxic contamination, and air pollution—are already beginning to slow economic and social progress in much of the world. . .

Building an environmentally stable future requires some vision of what it would look like. If not coal and oil to power society, then what? If forests are no longer to be cleared to grow food, then how is a larger population to be fed? If a throwaway culture leads inevitably to pollution and resource depletion, how can we satisfy our material needs?

In sum, if the present path is so obviously unsound, what picture of the future can we use to guide our actions toward a global community that can endure?

A sustainable society is one that satisfies its needs without jeopardizing the prospects of future generations. Unfortunately, no models of sustainability exist today. Most developing nations have for the past several decades aspired to the automobile-centered, fossil-fuel-driven economies of the industrial West. From the regional problems of air pollution to the global threat of climate change, though, it is clear that these societies are far from durable; indeed, they are rapidly bringing about their own demise. . .

Time to get the world on the sustainable path is rapidly running out. We believe that if humanity achieves sustainability, it will do so within the next 40 years. If we have not succeeded by then, environmental deterioration and economic decline will be feeding on each other, pulling us down toward social decay and political upheaval. At such a point, reclaiming any hope of a sustainable future might be impossible. Our vision, therefore, looks to the year 2030, a time closer to the present than is World War II. . .

Begin with the Basics

In attempting to sketch the outlines of a sustainable society, we need to make some basic assumptions. First, our vision of the future assumes only existing technologies and foreseeable improvements in them. This clearly is a conservative assumption: 40 years ago, for example, some renewable energy technologies on which we base our model didn't even exist.

Second, the world economy of 2030 will not be powered by

Illustration by Carol*Simpson

coal, oil and natural gas. It is now well accepted that continuing heavy reliance on fossil fuels will cause catastrophic changes in climate. . .

The third major assumption is about population size. Current United Nations projections have the world headed for nearly nine billion people by 2030. This figure implies a doubling or tripling of the populations of Ethiopia, India, Nigeria, and scores of other countries where human numbers are already overtaxing natural support systems. But such growth is inconceivable. Either these societies will move quickly to encourage smaller families and bring birthrates down, or rising death rates from hunger and malnutrition will check population growth.

The human path to sustainability by the year 2030 therefore requires a dramatic drop in birthrates. As of this year, 13 European countries had stable or declining populations; by 2030, most countries are likely to be in that category. We assume a population 40 years from now of at most eight billion that will be either essentially stable or declining slowly toward a number the earth can comfortably support.

Dawn of a Solar Age

In many ways, the solar age today is where the coal age was when the steam engine was invented in the 18th century. At that time, coal was used to heat homes and smelt iron ore, but the notion of using coal-fired steam engines to power factories or transportation systems was just emerging. Only a short time later, the first railroad started running and fossil fuels began to transform the world economy.

Many technologies have been developed that allow us to harness the renewable energy of the sun effectively, but so far these devices are only in limited use. By 2030 they will be widespread and much improved. The pool of energy these technologies can tap is immense: the annual influx of accessible renewable resources in the United States is estimated at 250 times the country's current energy needs. . .

Efficient in All Senses

Getting total global carbon emissions down to two billion tons a year will require vast improvements in energy efficiency. Fortunately, many of the technologies to accomplish this feat already exist and are cost-effective. No technical breakthroughs are needed to double automobile fuel economy, triple the efficiency of lighting systems, or cut typical home heating requirements by 75 percent.

Automobiles in 2030 are apt to get at least 100 miles per gallon of fuel, four times the current average for new cars. A hint of what such vehicles may be like is seen in the Volvo LCP 2000, a recently developed prototype automobile. It is an aerodynamic four-passenger car that weighs half as much as today's models. Moreover, it has a highly efficient and clean-burning diesel engine. With the addition of a continuously variable transmission and a flywheel energy storage device, this vehicle will get 90 miles to the gallon. . .

How to Feed Eight Billion

Imagine trying to meet the food, fuel, and timber needs of eight billion people—nearly three billion more than the current population—with 960 billion fewer tons of topsoil (more than twice the amount on all U.S. cropland) and one billion fewer acres of trees (an area more than half the size of the continental

United States).

That, in a nutshell, will be the predicament faced by society in 2030 if current rates of soil erosion and deforestation continue unaltered for the next 40 years. It is a fate that can only be avoided through major changes in land use.

Of necessity, societies in 2030 will be using the land intensively; the needs of a population more than half again as large as today's cannot be met otherwise. But, unlike the present, tomorrow's land-use patterns would be abiding by basic principles of biological stability: nutrient retention, carbon balance, soil protection, water conservation, and preservation of species diversity. Harvests will rarely exceed sustainable yields.

It seems inevitable that adequately nourishing a world population 60 percent larger than today's will preclude feeding a third of the global grain harvest to livestock and poultry, as is currently the case. As meat becomes more expensive, the diets of the affluent will move down the food chain to greater consumption of grains and vegetables, which will also prolong lifespans.

A Healthy Respect for Forests

Forests and woodlands will be valued more highly and for many more reasons in 2030 than is the case today. The planet's mantle of trees, already a third smaller than in pre-agricultural times and shrinking by more than 27 million acres per year now, will be stable or expanding as a result of serious efforts to slow deforestation and to replant vast areas.

Long before 2030, the clearing of most tropical forests will have ceased. Since most of the nutrients in these ecosystems are held in the leaves and biomass of the vegetation rather than in the soil, only activities that preserve the forest canopy are sustainable. While it is impossible to say how much virgin tropical forest would remain in 2030 if sustainability is achieved, certainly the rate of deforestation will have had to slow dramatically by the end of this decade. Soon thereafter it will come to a halt. . .

Restoring and stabilizing the biological resource base by 2030 depends on a pattern of land ownership and use far more equitable than today's. Much of the degradation now occurring stems from the heavily skewed distribution of land that, along with population growth, pushes poor people into ever more marginal environments. Stewardship requires that people have plots large enough to sustain their families without abusing the land, access to means of using the land productively, and the right to pass it on to their children. . .

Economic Progress in a New Light

The fundamental changes that are needed in energy, forestry, agriculture, and other physical systems cannot occur without corresponding shifts in social, economic, and moral character. During the transition to sustainability, political leaders and citizens alike will be forced to reevaluate their goals and aspirations and to adjust to a new set of principles that have at their core the welfare of future generations.

Shifts in employment will be among the most visible as the transition gets under way. Moving from fossil fuels to a diverse set of renewable energy sources, extracting fewer materials from the earth and recycling more, and revamping farming and forestry practices will greatly expand co-opportunities in new areas. Job losses in coal mining, auto production, and metals prospecting will be offset by gains in the manufacture and sale of photovoltaic solar cells, wind turbines, bicycles, mass transit equipment, and a host of technologies for recycling materials.

Since planned obsolescence will itself be obsolete in a sustainable society, a far greater share of workers will be employed in repair, maintenance, and recycling activities than in the extraction of virgin materials and production of new goods.

A New Set of Values

Movement toward a lasting society cannot occur without a transformation of individual priorities and values. Throughout the ages, philosophers and religious leaders have denounced materialism as a path to human fulfillment. Yet societies across the ideological spectrum have persisted in equating quality of life with increased consumption.

Because of the strain on resources it creates, materialism simply cannot survive the transition to a sustainable world. As public understanding of the need to adopt simpler and less consumptive lifestyles spreads, it will become unfashionable to own fancy new cars, clothes and the latest electronic devices. The potential benefits of unleashing the human energy now devoted to producing, advertising, buying, consuming, and discarding material goods are enormous.

As the amassing of personal and national wealth becomes less of a goal, the gap between haves and have-nots will gradually close, eliminating many societal tensions. Ideological differences may fade as well, as nations adopt sustainability as a common cause, and as they come to recognize that achieving it requires a shared set of values that includes democratic principles, freedom to innovate, respect for human rights, and acceptance of diversity. With the cooperative tasks involved in repairing the earth so many and so large, the idea of waging war could become an anachronism.

The task of building a sustainable society is an enormous one that will take decades rather than years. Indeed, it is an undertaking that will easily absorb the energies that during the past 40 years have been devoted to the Cold War. The reward in the year 2030 could be an Earth Day with something to celebrate: the achievement of a society in balance with the resources that support it, instead of one that destroys the underpinnings of its future.

28 PUBLIC POLICY AND CLIMATE CHANGE

FREE MARKET VALUES WILL PROTECT THE ENVIRONMENT

Fred Smith

Fred Smith is President of the Competitive Enterprise Institute, a classical liberal think tank based in Washington, D.C., and a leading advocate of free market solutions to environmental problems.

Points to Consider:

1. Explain the meaning of free market environmentalism.

2. Why did the market protect American cattle?

3. What is the government's role in environmental concerns?

4. How have environmental groups harmed the environment?

5. How can free market environmentalism help save the environment?

"Free Market Environmentalism: An Interview with Fred Smith," Competitive Enterprise Institute, April, 1990, in the newsletter, *Organizational Trends.*

*There's a strange failure to address what the
evidence shows, which is that market oriented
societies do a very good job in the environmental
area.*

What exactly is free market environmentalism?

Free market environmentalism is an alternative approach to
addressing environmental issues, recognizing that those parts of
the world that have the freest economies have also been most
successful in protecting their environment. Those areas of the
world that have had the most regulated, government-controlled
economies have also had the greatest environmental disasters.
The most government-controlled, most regulated economy in the
world, the Soviet Union, has seen the greatest and to date the
only really serious nuclear disaster: Chernobyl. What is the
lesson? Increased power meant decreased accountability; the
state's interests overrode those of the citizens. And yet, the
conclusion reached in the United States is that we need more
government controls and regulation.

What free market environmentalists are trying to do is to find
ways of extending the marketplace to those resources now at
risk so that doing a good job in the economy means doing a
good job in the ecology, and vice versa.

The African elephant gives us a classic example. The
traditional view, the view of the anti-market environmental wing,
has been that higher prices for elephant ivory have created the
threat to the African elephant, and therefore we must suppress
the market to safeguard the elephant.

Unfortunately, elephants have been largely left out of the
ownership system in most of Africa. In those areas of Africa
(Zimbabwe, Botswana, South Africa, Lesotho, and parts of
Zambia) where the elephant is owned, higher prices have led to
the local people being able to spend more money and more
time for protecting the elephant. People do better economically;
the elephant does better ecologically. Rather than a segregation
strategy, which tries to keep nature and man separated, we have
an integration strategy which brings the African elephant into the
world economy, and therefore allows the African elephant and
the African native both to do well.

So you see the environmentalist movement as essentially hostile to free market philosophy?

Hostile at the leadership level; naive at the membership level.
At the leadership level, one is dealing with individuals who are
part of the modern liberal movement, people who believe that if
there's a problem, one needs government action to resolve that
problem; and the environmental issue has become their major
way of achieving that effect. If socialism and collective action

are discredited in other parts of the economy and other parts of society, environmentalism becomes the last refuge for the true believer in a "government-knows-best" approach. . .

Do you see any role for government in environmental protection?

First, government should stop the subsidized destruction of the environment. The government should stop subsidizing the uneconomic cutting of trees, the uneconomic development of canals and dams and all of the public works projects that are not only wasteful from a taxpayer perspective, but are also environmentally disruptive. So there's a whole program of government doing less—less harm to the environment and less harm to the taxpayer.

Secondly, there's a need for government ultimately to privatize many areas where it is now playing a role: everything from trash collection and disposal to forestry to western water policy to western grazing lands. All those areas should be privatized. At the same time, it is critical that the government create and enforce property rights.

Beyond that, government should recognize that the laws that inhibit the development of private sector solutions should be rethought. There are many laws in America which prohibit private ownership. For example, one is not allowed to own an endangered species. As a result, just when a species of plant or animal most needs people who care about it and protect it, we cut off that product from the marketplace. There can be no ownership of that species.

Do you see any other encouraging signs right now; and, more specifically, on what issues do you think free market groups have the best chance?

Well, I think there are some encouraging signs. One of the causes for optimism is that the internal contradictions of ecological central planning are gradually beginning to create tensions and offer an opportunity to rethink. Power corrupts, and the modern environmental movement has so much power (the top 14 groups have over $200 million of resources and thousands of full-time staffers). This army of people is overwhelming any rational debate in this area. Because they have very little opposition, they've become muscle-bound hulks that don't think about what they're trying to do. They are making serious mistakes. They're arrogant, they're thoughtless, and they're doing things that are going to be destructive. They're going to pay a price for that.

Second, I think the business community is beginning to realize that this is a long-term ideological struggle, and that there is very little hope that the business community can survive the kind of world the leaders of the modern environmental

---

CAPITALISM AND THE ENVIRONMENT

One lesson that should have been obvious from Eastern Europe is that, despite what the Greens may think, private property and free enterprise are themselves very important environmental programs. Had Eastern Europe simply reached U.S. levels of energy and material efficiency, it would now face a far less serious environmental situation. Energy consumption per ton of steel, fertilizer applied per bushel of wheat, mileage incurred in producing final products—these and a host of other production statistics reflect the superiority of capitalism in realizing a more efficient and less pollution-intensive economy.

Update, *Competitive Enterprise Institute Newsletter, March, 1990*

---

movement would like to see.

Third, the free market community, which has been growing over the last decade especially, is now beginning to focus on environmental policies. The Earth Day Alternative work that we're doing provides a starting point. Groups such as the Political Economy Research Center and the Institute of Political Economy have been working in the natural resource area for almost a decade. Now they're expanding into pollution control areas and some of the other critical environmental areas. Other groups which have not been involved in this area, at least in any consistent way, such as the Reason Foundation, the Pacific Research Institute, the Heritage Foundation, and CATO are getting more involved.

How do you think free market groups have been doing in addressing environmental issues?

We are beginning to learn how to creatively engage the debate, but we've got to do much more. The whole conservative movement has to take environmental policy seriously. Right now, the arguments in favor of free markets are that free markets are wonderful. They produce a lot of great things. There's just one little problem: they endanger the future of the world. Well, that's a pretty big problem. If that really is true, then we should be questioning markets.

It's not true. We have not been aggressive enough about explaining that, and explaining what is endangering the world, which is that far too much of the world economy is under political control. We need to tell the stories about the African elephants, about the salmon streams in Scotland where fishing rights owners are able to play a positive role in protecting the environment because they care about their fish.

We need to talk about the potential for shell fisheries being owned, and therefore having people worried about water pollution directly when it occurs, acting as early tripwires for possible coastal pollution.

We need to talk about moving away from a national technology standard in the air pollution area to converting gasoline taxes and registration fees, which serve no useful purpose, into pollution fees. You would have an automobile tested, rated by its pollution per mile potential, its mileage reading read and then at the end of the year a fee would be calculated, based on the pollution potential of that car times the miles that it's been driven. So each polluter pays for the amount of pollution he's contributing. Houses are treated that way. Most people now live in homes that have electric meters, water meters, gas meters, telephone meters, cable television meters on occasion. We pay for each of those services to the extent we use them. If an automobile were thought of that way, we would have a pollution meter in our car, and we would begin to pay for the amount of pollution we produce.

We need to find ways of making pollution part of the everyday cost of living our lives. As we do so, we'll take account of it in a serious way rather than in this frivolous way we're doing now.

Environmental policy needs to be taken seriously. Which means that we should try to enlist the same system which has done so well at producing food, housing, and lifestyles in the Western world and apply it to environmental amenities. To turn over environment management to the kind of system which failed to produce wheat in the Soviet Union would be criminal.

BIBLIOGRAPHY

American Council for an Energy-Efficient Economy. Energy Efficiency: A New Agenda, by William V. Chandler, Howard S. Geller, and Marc R. Ledbetter. Washington, 1988. 76 p.

Crosson, Pierre. Greenhouse Warming and Climate Change: Why Should We Care? *Food Policy,* v. 14, no. 2, May 1989: 107-118.

Ellsaesser, Hugh W. and S. Fred Singer. The Greenhouse Effect: Science Fiction? *Consumers' Research,* v. 71, November 1988: 27-33.

George C. Marshall Institute. Scientific Perspectives on the Greenhouse Problem, by Frederick Seitz, Robert Jastrow, and William A. Nierenberg. Washington, 1989. 37 p.

Getting Warmer—Should We Worry? *Journal of Policy Analysis and Management,* v. 7, spring 1988: 425-475.

Hoffman, John S. and Michael J. Gibbs. Future Concentrations of Stratospheric Chlorine and Bromine. EPA 400/1-88/005. August 1988.

Jaeger, Jill. Developing Policies for Responding to Climate Change: A Summary of Discussions and Recommendations of the Workshop Held in Villach (Sept. 28-Oct. 20, 1987) and Bellagio (Nov. 9-13, 1987), Under the Auspices of the Beijer Institute, Stockholm. [s.l.] World Meteorological Organization, 1988. 53 p.

Postel, Sandra. Global View of a Tropical Disaster. *American Forests,* v. 94, November-December 1988: 25-29, 69-71.

Putnam, Hayes & Bartlett, Inc. Economic Implications of Potential Chlorofluorocarbon Restrictions. Dec. 2, 1987. Available from Alliance for Responsible CFC Policy.

Ray, Dixy Lee. The Greenhouse Blues: Keep Cool about Global Warming. *Policy Review,* summer 1989: 70-72.

Schneider, Stephen H. Climate Modeling. *Scientific American,* May 1987: 72-78, 80.

———Doing Something about the Weather. *World Monitor,* v. 1, December 1988: 28-37.

Scientific American (entire issue). *Managing Planet Earth.*

September 1989. 190 p. (special issue).

Shepard, Michael, et al. The Politics of Climate. *EPRI Journal*, June 1988: 4-15.

Smit, B., L. Ludlow, and M. Brklacich. Implications of a Global Climatic Warming for Agriculture: A Review and Appraisal. *Journal of Environmental Quality*, v. 17, October-December 1988: 519-527.

The Oceans and Global Warming. *Oceanus* (entire issue), v. 32, no. 2, summer 1989: 96.

U.S. Department of Energy. Energy Information Administration. Potential Costs of Restricting Chlorofluorocarbon Use. August 1989.

U.S. Congress. Committee on Agriculture. Subcommittees on Department Operations, Research, and Foreign Agriculture and on Forests, Family Farms, and Energy. Hearing, 101st Congress, 1st session. Apr. 19, 1989. Washington, U.S. Govt. Print Off., 1990. 150 p. "Serial no. 101-28"

U.S. Congress. House. Committee on Appropriations. Subcommittee on Foreign Operations, Export Financing, and Related Programs. Export financing, and programs appropriations for 1990. Part 4: Environmental issues. Hearings, 101st Congress, 1st session. Feb. 21, 1989. Washington, U.s. Govt. Print. Off., 1989. 670 p.

U.S. Congress. House. Committee on Energy and Commerce. Subcommittee on Energy and Power. Global Warming. Hearings, 101st Congress, 1st session. Feb. 21 and May 4, 1989. Washington, U.S, Govt. Print. Off., 1989. 177 p. "Serial no. 101-31"

U.S. Congress. House. Committee on Merchant Marine and Fisheries. Subcommittee on Oceanography and the Great Lakes. Global Climate Change. Hearing, 101st Congress, 1st session, on H.R. 980. May 4, 1989. Washington, U.S. Govt. Print. Off., 1989. 165 p. "Serial no. 101-15"

– – –Global Environmental Research and Policy Act of 1989; report to accompany H.R. 3332. Dec. 15, 1989. Washington, U.S. Govt. Print. Off., 1989. 22 p. (101st Congress, 1st session. House. Report no. 101-394, part 1)

U.S. Congress. House. Committee on Science, Space and Technology. Subcommittees on Natural Resources, Agriculture Research and Environment and on International Scientific

Cooperation. Hearing, 101st Congress, 1st session. July 27, 1989. Washington, U.S. Govt. Print. Off., 1990. 280 p.

U.S. Congress. Senate. Committee on Agriculture, Nutrition, and Forestry. Agriculture, Forestry, and Global Climate Change—a Reader. Prepared by the Congressional Research Service, Library of Congress. Washington, U.S. Govt. Print. Off., April 1989. 618 p.

At head of title: 101st Congress, 1st session. Committee print (S.Rpt. 101-26).

U.S. Congress. Senate. Committee on Commerce, Science, and Transportation. National Global Change Research Act of 1989. Hearing, 101st Congress, 1st session, on S. 169. Feb. 22, 1989. Washington, U.S. Govt. Print. Off., 1989. 185 p.

— — —National Global Change Research Act of 1989. May 31, 1989. Washington, 1989. 25 p. (101st Congress, 1st session. Senate. Report no. 101-40)

— — —National Ocean Policy Study, Global Change—An Ocean Perspective. Hearing, 101st Congress, 1st session. Apr. 11,, 1989. Washington, U.S. Govt. Print. Off., 1989. 81 p. (S.Hrg. 101-95)

U.S. Congress. Senate. Committee on Commerce, Science, and Transportation. Subcommittee on Science, Technology, and Space. Climate Surprises. Hearing, 101st Congress, 1st session, on possible climate surprises—predicting greenhouse warming. May 8, 1989. Washington, U.S. Govt. Print. Off., 1989. (S.Hrg. 101-128) 152 p.

U.S. Congress. Senate. Committee on Energy and Natural Resources. DOE's National Energy Plan and Global Warming. Hearing, 101st Congress, 1st session, on the formulation of a national energy plan and related policies which affect global climate change. July 26, 1989. Washington, U.S. Govt. Print. Off., 1989. 155 p. (S.Hrg. 101-235)

U.S, Congress. Senate. Committee on Environment and Public Works. Subcommittee on Environmental Protection. Policy options for stabilizing global climate. Hearing, 101st Congress, 1st session. Mar. 17, 1989. Washington, U.S. Govt. Print. Off., 1989. 69 p. (S.Hrg. 101-31)

U.S. Library of Congress. Congressional Research Service. Controlling Carbon Dioxide Emissions, by Amy Abel, Mark E. Holt, and Larry B. Parker. Mar. 9, 1989. [Washington] 1989. 34 p. CRS Report 89-157 ENR

— — —Ethanol Fuel and Global Warming, by Migdon Segal. Mar. 6, 1989. [Washington] 1989. 18 p. *CRS Report* 89-164 SPR

— — —National Climate Program: Background and Implementation, by John R. Justus and Robert E. Morrison. Mar. 31, 1988. [Washington] 1988. 72 p. *CRS Report* 88-289 SPR

— — —The Global Environment. *CRS Review* (entire issue). [Washington] August 1989.

— — —The Unpredictable Atmosphere: Selected References, by Karen L. Alderson. January 1990. [Washington] 1990. 32 p.

World Resources Institute. A Matter of Degrees: The Potential for Controlling the Greenhouse Effect, Irving M. Mintzer. Washington, 1987. 60 p. (Research Report no. 5)

U.S. Office of Science and Technology Policy. Federal Coordinating Council on Science, Engineering and Technology. Committee on the Earth Sciences. Our Changing Planet: The FY 1990 Research Plan (the U.S. Global Change Research Program). [Washington] July 1989. 183 p.

Zurer, Pamela S. Chemists Solve Key Puzzle of Antarctic Ozone Hole. *Chemical and Engineering News*, Nov. 30, 1987: 25-27.

— — —Producers, Users Grapple with Realities of CFC Phaseout. *Chemical and Engineering News*, July 24, 1989: 7-13.